Ninique

THE
RELATIONSHIP
REVOLUTION

Welcome to The
Revolution

Blessings
Owen

THE RELATIONSHIP REVOLUTION

ARE YOU PART OF
THE MOVEMENT OR PART
OF THE RESISTANCE?

OWEN WILLIAMS

Published in 2009 by
BPS Books
Toronto, Canada
www.bpsbooks.com
A division of
Bastian Publishing Services Ltd.

ISBN 978-1-926645-04-9

Canadian Cataloguing in Publication Data available from
Library and Archives Canada

Cover design: Robin Uchida
Text design and typesetting: Tannice Goddard, Soul Oasis Networking

Printed by Lightning Source, Tennessee. Lightning Source paper, as used in this book, does not come from endangered old growth forests or forests of exceptional conservation value. It is acid free, lignin free, and meets all ANSI standards for archival-quality paper. The print-on-demand process used to produce this book protects the environment by printing only the number of copies that are purchased.

To Ali,
my beloved co-conspirator
on this journey of life

Contents

Preface

FOR MANY YEARS I HAD a mentor who conducted her life from a slow and grounded place. She lived with great health until she was almost one hundred and two. She had no children, though she was married twice — her second marriage lasting forty-five years. Mrs. Lillie taught and inspired me to slow down and focus on what matters most. She was fond of telling me that the answers are inside us; that if we can just get out of our own way and slow ourselves down long enough for our bodies to catch up with us, all would be revealed. "You can't figure things out in your head," she often said. "Get into your body and get them working together."

I have written this book in service of the countless people who have crossed my path both personally and professionally and have shared their desire for what I, too, have always wanted: a simpler life — the kind of life Mrs. Lillie modeled for me. I have always known that there was an easier way to be in the world; indeed, in many respects my parents, while far from perfect, lived a simpler way. This book in part is about returning to what has always been, a return to the innocent in each of us where life just is. A place where there is no angst but simply peace.

For many years I have pondered the questions:

- What if the relationship I have with myself is the key to what I create with others?
- What if life really could be this simple?
- What would I have to let go of to create peace in my life?
- What if the way I've chosen to see my world is really just a dream?
- What would I create for myself if I could dream a different dream?

This book is a result of my exploration of these questions; it is my attempt to meet a desire felt by most of us to create the kind of relationships and families that will collectively co-create a healthier community at large. The book is based on two major principles: that we have to get out of our own way and that relationship is a vehicle for our greatness.

Although this book is written in the context of conventional marriage, the principles may be applied to all relationships.

Acknowledgments

MY HEARTFELT THANKS go out to my sister Shân Hughes, who went out of her way to support me in the writing of this book. And to my coach, Tony Parry, whose love and wisdom are priceless. I also choose to acknowledge myself for the courage to step in and make this happen. I would never have started to write this book if I had known what it would take to complete it, yet I have grown immensely through committing to bring it to life.

There are many special people along the way who have been there for me and without whose feedback and insight I wouldn't have gained the strength needed for this task. A big thank-you to Don Bastian and his team at BPS Books. In no particular order I want to thank Boris Krul, Lianne Doucet, Jennifer Pernfuss, Chris and Nikki St. John, Eileen Daly, Fran and Dermot Grove-White, Anne-Shirley Clough, Paul Vereshak, Simon Mortimer, Karen and Henry Kimsey-House, Thiaga Murugasu, and Sue Pimento.

And for their creativity I celebrate Lorraine Parow and Robin Uchida, who without doubt enhance beauty in the world.

Introduction

MANY OF US AT ONE time or another have asked ourselves, "What am I doing in this relationship?" This question is usually a precursor to an intense desire to end the relationship by running away from the tension of the moment.

Indeed, relationships in our society are as disposable as a fast-food container. Many of us try to solve our current relationship problem by getting into a new relationship. Others of us stay, but we might as well have thrown our relationship away. For us, relationship fatigue has set in. Tired of getting hurt, we settle for whatever we can get — usually a bland, mediocre existence that passes for relationship.

Happy, healthy relationships are few and far between. For example, with the divorce rate in Canada at over fifty percent, an estimated 50,000 children were impacted by divorce in 2008 alone. The numbers are tragic and getting worse. At least eighty percent of the couples I coach through relationship challenges are themselves from divorced families. The tone set for them then and intensified today is that divorce is not just an acceptable option, it's mainstream.

We need a Relationship Revolution, and we need it now. A revolution that would cause us to ask the question above with the emphasis on the "I" — indicating that we take responsibility for the tone and quality of our relationship.

Whether we're dealing in our relationship with infidelity, anger issues, setting and maintaining boundaries, self-care, money, work, sex, in-laws, or any other issue, we face a choice point. Do we stick with the boring, unfulfilling "devil" of a relationship we know; get out of the relationship altogether; or deepen our commitment to the relationship we're in by working on ourselves?

I have coached individuals and couples for over fifteen years and have come to the conclusion that relationships are innocent until proven guilty. Unless one member of the couple is aggressing against the other and is absolutely unwilling to change, it is better for the couple to deepen their learning of themselves within their present relationship. I tell them they get to deal with their challenges now in their present relationship or find themselves in another problematic relationship. Because even if a woman thinks she keeps attracting "the wrong kind of man," that is her issue. Or if a man thinks "women only want one thing," that is his issue to explore and resolve. The only thing we need to change in life is our mind.

People leave a relationship out of reaction, anger, and frustration, projecting on the other all that they didn't do or needed to do for the relationship to work. We have become fixated on blaming and finding fault in relationship. We are only too happy to focus on what the other person is doing (or not doing), using this to justify our own frustrations within the relationship. Or we become so fixated on ourselves and what *we're* not doing that we turn our criticism inward and feel trapped.

A recurring theme in my practice has been the number of men and women who are still living with regret or self-doubt about their decision to end a past relationship. I am often asked by them, and also by those who are considering taking the same course of action, "How do you know when it's the right time to leave a relationship?"

I always answer that the mere fact of asking the question means it isn't the right time. "You will know the right time to leave because you will feel peaceful in your body," I say. "You will be with the deeper realization that you have done everything within your power to set a tone and intention for yourself in the relationship and for your partner to join you there. Setting the tone is a courageous and loving act. For you and your partner. You will be tested when you finally choose to step in in this way."

Think about it. If things have been going along less than desirably in your relationship and you decide to change the rules of the system that you have co-created, the other person isn't all of a sudden going to throw their arms around you and proclaim their undying love for you for finally stepping up to the plate. No, they are going to criticize, resist, resent, and challenge you to see if you are willing to stay in the tension of their truth and stay grounded in the process. Someone has to be a rock in the process and hold out the possibility of something better.

Once we finally choose to step in, we will meet our own edge, which we will have to grow through. Only in this space in the relationship will we be able to determine our partner's willingness to join us. It is a choice every step of the way. If they choose not to meet us there and we know deep within that we have done everything we can to open a sacred space for the other to meet us, we can step through to the other side in a loving way. Yes, there will be sadness and disappointment on both sides for the loss of what we had hoped for. There is also a freedom in our knowing our deeper truth.

We are brought to this choice point over and over again. It is important to see, however, that the interplay of any conflict in relationships has very little to do with what the couple, or the individuals, for that matter, are experiencing in the moment. Difficult though this concept may be for us to grasp, the conflict we are in is connected to patterns of behaviors and beliefs set up within us long before we knew the other existed on the planet.

If you think what's going on in your life as a couple has little to do with your past, think again.

I worked with a young woman whose father was a wealthy, self-made businessman. She and her sister had been told they would each receive a million pounds on their wedding day. They lived in a swank house in London, England, complete with in-ground pool and gardener and a choice of five high-end cars to drive. They had a horse farm and an exquisite cottage.

From the outside it appeared this young woman was living a charmed life. However, she grew up with a large dose of distrust, picking up from her father that "it's a dog-eat-dog world; you have to get them before they get you." She saw how money dominated her father's life and how desperately unhappy her mother was in their relationship.

As a result, this young woman didn't trust the men she dated and ultimately didn't trust herself. She was not aware of her own value as a woman. Dating was hellish for her and she became both drug and alcohol addicted right under her parents' noses. She needed to leave the cocoon of "safety" her parents were giving her but didn't have the wherewithal to make it on her own.

Any guesses as to the patterns she brought to a relationship? And her subsequent relationships? She projected her distrust on each and every man thereafter. Her work was to trust her deeper truth and live from there.

I worked with a man whose father wouldn't give him or his sister any money. Children should work for every penny they earned, was his recurrent sermon. His mother snuck money to them, always with the words, "Don't tell your father." As an adult, he distrusted women, living out the story that all women lie to men. He interrogated his partners to uncover their lies, and they soon fell prey to his script. One of his girlfriends told me, "If he's going to constantly accuse me of lying, even when I'm telling the truth, then I might as well lie." Ah the delicious trap of a self-fulfilling prophecy! This man was serially unsuccessful in his relationships.

Many people see relationship and marriage as a restriction of their freedom. This is based on their evaluation of other relationships they have experienced or witnessed. This is one of the central ways that people perpetuate their singleness or misery within their relationship. They hide behind sentiments like, "Better the devil you know than the devil you don't." Now that's hopeful! Or they decide to "grin and bear it," co-existing by "walking on eggshells." It's no wonder they feel trapped.

The Revolution

What is the Relationship Revolution that I am urging as a solution to such issues?

This revolution is every bit as radical in relationships as the Copernican Revolution was in astronomy. The Relationship Revolution holds that we must shift from a geocentric view, in which we see our relationship as revolving around us, to a heliocentric view, in which we see ourselves as revolving around our relationship. And just as the Copernican Revolution set the stage for a more accurate, applicable, and productive view of scientific reality, so the Relaltionship Revolution will bring us to a deeper and more fulfilling understanding of ourselves and the way we relate.

Joining this movement requires a fundamental shift. Instead of feeling that the relationship isn't satisfying us as individuals, we must understand that the relationship defines us — together and as individuals.

The Relationship Revolution brings to light and reveals to us the impact of our family of origin, primarily our parents, on our current relationship. We either cannot see these effects — or we see them and feel trapped by them.

As infants, our parents represent the world to us. As we grow and develop, our world expands from our mother and father's loving arms to our crib and playpen, then to the safety of the living-room floor, our high chair, and so on. Our world keeps getting bigger, and we adjust to the information we get about our world through our family, friends, schooling, and life experiences. The book of our life fills in quickly. Our parents teach us what a loving relationship is by modeling one for us. Whether their model is good, bad, or indifferent, we learn our reality from them.

All families operate within an inherited system regardless of whether it was composed of one parent, or two, or was a blended family. And any current relationship operates within a system based on the systems brought to it by the people in the relationship.

When a new relationship forms between a couple, the two family systems that they represent collide, often leading to conflict. Expectations flow from each family system, represented as rules, sometimes spoken and often unspoken and invisible especially to someone outside the system. Once we engage in a relationship, we are engaging in the family system rules imposed by our partner's family. One of the rules is that the rules cannot be challenged. Challenging the rules can evoke as drastic a response as shunning or ridicule. The impact of these responses breeds several options: rebellion, complacency, or low-grade disconnection. The deep fear that governs our compliance with the rules is our fear that love and approval will be withdrawn.

These are the same experiences we have to face as we develop in a romantic relationship, or any other relationship for that matter. When two family systems are on a collision course, conflict and tension inevitably arise. Because we're lousy at hanging out in the tension that different feelings bring and understanding them, we exit the relationship by staying at work longer than we need, by spending hours playing video games, reading, searching the Internet, and living on our BlackBerry. Because of this inability to hang out in the tension, we make life-altering decisions early in a relationship: "I can't go there or say that"; "there's no point in arguing — it doesn't change a thing"; "what's the point?"

I know of a couple who had a fight in their first month together. Each one privately vowed never to fight again because it was "too painful." They ended up living empty, parallel lives. I know of other couples who became so entrenched in conflict that fighting was how they connected. They moved from battle to battle in an attempt to create intimacy.

In all such cases, the individuals involved are expecting the relationship to revolve around them. They fail to see that they are revolving around the relationship in an orbit that is co-created; that they ultimately get to decide how they want their dance to play out; that each of them exists to strengthen the relationship they are in — and that *this* is how they will become strong as individuals and create the connection we all long for.

Joining the movement does require a deeper knowledge of self. The revolutionary part, however, is that the relationship becomes the catalyst of our own individual growth and potential. The relationship is a co-created dance with another that brings forth joy, peace, and simplicity of being. Inside this dance is also conflict. In the revolution, conflict is seen as a gift because it reveals to us the material we need to work through and grow from.

We have to be willing to de-role our parents and see them as human beings with their own limitations and foibles. How much do we really know about the way they were shaped, influenced, and impacted by their life experiences?

I learned the most about my parents in my forties, when I became fascinated with how I had been influenced to become the person I was. I learned about family secrets and how they shaped the landscape. I learned that my father was incomplete with his own father before he died. That my mother was told by her mother she could never return home if she married my father, a statement that informed many of the decisions she made in her marriage.

The Relationship Revolution transforms relationships by revealing these systems that we bring to relationship so we can develop a new life-giving system that strengthens each member of the relationship individually. This is why I describe the process as getting out of our own way and into the relationship we really want. As couples seek to understand their relationship, they will understand the relationships that made them. Understanding how they have been shaped will give them full choice about how they are evolving in relationship. "Children follow your footsteps, not your finger," my mother often said. It is no wonder that we are a product of our past. This is our situation to unravel, taking the best and leaving the rest, becoming what we truly want and taking responsibility for creating it.

Relationship is a dance of joy and discovery. In fact, like children, we learn best when we're having fun. As you read this book, you will learn how to get serious about your relationship and lighten up, whether the topic is relationship excellence, the work of men, women, and relationships, or how we can align our words and actions. Within this book you will be asked powerful questions. You will be given the opportunity to share your insights on the Website relationshipexcellence.com and to read other people's insights there.

Just to be clear, this journey is a journey of courage. The word *courage* has its origin in the French word *coeur*, which means *heart*. If you feel discouraged in your life and relationships, chances are you have lost heart. The Relationship Revolution is designed to encourage you to reconnect with your heart, have the courage to tell yourself the truth, face and overcome your fears (which aren't real anyway), and do things you may have never done before.

There isn't any point in going on a journey half-heartedly. Please, throw yourself in; after all, it is your life that you stand to gain.

1

The Revolution
Relationships are simple, not necessarily easy

RELATIONSHIPS TODAY AREN'T WORKING. Not for lack of desire or trying. There is a deep longing for change and a proliferation of self-help books, relationship courses, and even Web pages pointing people to a new awareness. These are not enough, however. Nothing short of a revolution is needed to rouse us from our deep sleep. Relationships need to be turned on their head. The old rules need to be thrown out the window. We have to reinvent, recycle, and renovate a system that is flawed. We have the opportunity to be courageous and take risks. We need to be willing to get comfortable with failure and recovery, learning about ourselves with a deep curiosity. It all begins with us.

Most people are driving down the street of their life with their eyes firmly fixed on the rear-view mirror. It's impossible to navigate our future while we are focused on our past. It is time for us to wake up, and not tomorrow but today! We change only when we're sick and tired of the results we're getting from being the way we are. We as individuals are the ones who have to choose something different for our lives and step into the uncertainty of tomorrow. We all have a need for certainty. Thus we trick ourselves into thinking we know what the future will bring. Yet in reality we have no idea what challenges life will present to us in the morning.

So why not invite the change we want into our lives today? The truth is, only we can do it; only we can be the catalyst of our own change. However, we cannot do it alone. We need others in our lives to assist and guide us through the process of self-awareness and into the greatness of who we are. For many of us, things must fall apart: We will be alerted to the necessity of change only once we reach our lowest of lows. Breakdown comes before breakthrough. It is as if we are a jigsaw puzzle and some of our pieces have been forced into the wrong spots. We need to pull them apart before we can put them together in a way that works.

This is where relationship comes into play. Relating to another person is how we discover our character traits, our behaviors, and our coping mechanisms. The rules that we have been brought up with are always being revealed to us. How we work with them is up to us.

And further, many of us will have to discover how we're stuck, caught up in the how to change, not understanding that we don't need to know how, we just have to be willing — the knowing comes later. We don't even need to know the way. The way knows the way. Once we are willing, it will present itself to us.

The state of the union

We live in the best of times and the worst of times when it comes to relationships between the sexes. Although we have unparalleled freedom to define gender roles and responsibilities, couple by couple, we have done great damage to certain realities.

For example, the concept of what it means to be a man in our culture is creating insanity. On the one hand, men, and especially dads, are portrayed in the popular media as fools or bumbling idiots, incapable of doing anything right. On the other hand, they are portrayed, by the same media, as superheroes who are deeply desirable to women, as magical beings with good looks, sculpted bodies, super-human powers, and no overt feelings. This fundamental confusion over the definition of what it means to be a man is directly contributing to the ineffectiveness of the modern relationship.

As for women, most have been led to think they're the experts when it comes to relationships. They tell themselves — supported by media myths — that they know what makes relationships work. As a result, they are entrusted with the responsibility, which they resent, of maintaining relationships. This stance perpetuates the myth that men are lousy at relationships; that they're just not willing to do the work required to maintain them; and that men themselves are the problem.

Women thirst for a relationship that meets their expectations. They believe those expectations will be met if they can fix men — or better yet motivate men to fix themselves. However, because men are no longer aware of their own identity, they are not ready to conform to expectations imposed by women and society as a whole. The real issue is the failure to see that men aren't broken. There is nothing to fix!

The flight from maturity

What's behind these relationship problems? The fact that most of us, men and women alike, have failed to take responsibility for our transition into adulthood. We are children masquerading as adults. The result? A marriage or relationship that cannot possibly work because it is composed of two adults behaving like children trying to solve adult issues. The real measure of maturity in a relationship is how we behave when we don't get our way with each other. Do we pout, withdraw, punish, and withhold our love and affection?

For confirmation that the child within us is most often in charge of the relationship, just look at the way we conduct ourselves in times of crisis, such as a divorce. Divorce often becomes a childlike battle based on raw emotion. The members of the couple gather their troops to support their own camp in defining and defiling the enemy. The battle of accusations is more reminiscent of a playground than a mature and once "loving" relationship. Lawyers are brought in to help fight the battle, but they often make a bad situation worse. They fall into the parental role, taking over the fight, setting the rules, and dictating the course of action.

How many highly skilled professionals who are successful in their career lead a miserable, unhappy, or unsatisfying personal life? The trouble is, most people, including professionals, may not have figured out how to manage their own lives properly, yet there they are impacting the lives of others with lasting effects. This is when the fights get downright dirty. The outcome is pure suffering: The family suffers, the man and the woman in the relationship suffer, their relationship suffers, and their children — not to mention in-laws and the extended family — suffer.

This is tragic, because a relationship is designed so its members may evolve, leaving them better off for having known each other rather than more hurt and wounded.

The transformational fire

We adults have failed to stand in the transformational fire that will forge us into well-rounded people who develop a trust of self, a crucial understanding of that self, and an awareness of who they are being. The good news is that a relationship — especially a marriage — is precisely the best opportunity for us to become acquainted with our own stuff, working through it in the loving presence of our partner on this journey of life.

Fifty years ago, we didn't have self-help books, encounter weekends, Webinars, and relationship therapists. There was nowhere near the level of specialization in every facet of the wide spectrum of relationship counseling and coaching. It was old school. Mothers talked to their daughters, imparting their wisdom and experience about relationships, dating, birthing, and men. Fathers guided boys into the ways of becoming men, husbands, and fathers. They taught them their role in the world and how to treat women. In other cases, people muddled through — and we all know how that has turned out.

We have lost the art of sharing within our families not only tradition but also ritual. As men we have lost the concept of what it means to be a "gentleman." That word has all but vanished from our language and experience. When I think of a gentleman, it conjures up the image of a secure, confident man who is clear in his beliefs and morals. A man who stands by his word, whose handshake means something. A man who shows respect, honor, and consideration. Where is this man and what happened to him? What happened to the guidance and teachings that made such a man?

We have lost respect for those teachings and even more so those teachers, whether we think of teachers in the traditional sense or as the fathers, elders, and others whose experience and life circumstances could benefit us tremendously. It is as if we feel we don't need or want to learn from others — as if we think we can get all the information we need from the Internet. With this know-it-all attitude, we close ourselves from what is really one of our most valuable sources of learning: others.

Commitment

We're in our own way, and the only way out is to gravitate toward someone who has developed mastery in the area we need to study and to submit ourselves to their teachings. We have to outgrow our own attitudes, and at a fundamental level this means growing up. We need to grow up! During this process of growth, we must look at the results we have in our lives as an indicator of what we're committed to. If we feel lonely, then that's what we're committed to. Instead of blaming others for our loneliness, we must look at how we're creating it.

I know a man who is a chronic complainer. Family members and friends alike move away from him. They ignore his calls and spend a great deal of energy to avoid connecting with him. This man cannot see how he is creating the disconnection. Sadly, no one has helped him take responsibility for, and change, his actions and therefore his results.

We can create change only from the understanding that what we have in our lives, in this moment, is what we are committed to. It is not *commitment* but *what we are committed to* that is the issue. If we're not sure what we're committed to, all we have to do is look at the results we're currently getting.

To create movement in your life, answer the following question:

What is present in your life? Conflict, loneliness, stagnation? In what way are you committed to this result?

To gain a deeper understanding, please go to relationshipexcellence.com to post your thoughts and read responses from others who are also committed to creating relationship excellence.

Taking responsibility

A revolution is created only when we're inspired to think. We have become lazy thinkers who want to be fed the answers to our problems. The Relationship Revolution requires us to take responsibility for the fact that the current model of relationship is not working.

I often ask the clients I'm coaching if they know how to make it with their partners. If they answer yes, I know we're in trouble because they're assuming they know what is best for the relationship. The truth is, we never really know how to make it with another. Relationship is a mystery that unfolds over time. We need to stop trying to control it. We need to admit that we don't know how to make it work, and that there isn't any one plan or template that will make it work. The only part we can control is the part we play.

How many couples do we know who have a relationship worth emulating? And if we do know one, would we have the courage to ask them how they got there and what they've learned about relating to each other in the process? Most of us don't ask because doing so would mean admitting our failure. We are, again, in our own way. If we don't ask, if we don't seek that knowledge, how can we ever succeed together?

Taking risks

There are two types of conversations: ones that take us nowhere and ones that take us somewhere.

Easy conversations, the kind we have with people day to day, are in the former category. Some of these conversations are born out of fear, keeping the connection on the surface to avoid going deeper to something of substance.

Difficult conversations take us somewhere because they are an act of taking responsibility. They help us grow and evolve. These conversations are vital if we want to move our life forward and deepen our awareness of who we really are. We learn and grow when we pull the real goods out of ourselves: the truth, the stuff that really matters. What we say in these difficult conversations may be as surprising to ourselves as to others.

There is inherent risk in revealing ourselves to ourselves, let alone in revealing ourselves to others: Once we have spoken our truth, we have a responsibility to bring it into being.

There is also risk in concealing who we are. If we're to live life full out, we have to accept risk. The main risk we face is "getting hurt." It is impossible to be in a relationship, even a flourishing one, and not get hurt. Getting hurt is part of the landscape. We get hurt because we misunderstand, misinterpret, and make assumptions.

This awareness or self-knowledge is crucial in our interaction with others. The degree to which we can create change and connection in relationships is directly proportional to the degree we risk.

We all make up stories. We leave a message for someone and they don't call us back. Or a loved one is hours late and hasn't called. What do we do? We create a story to help us deal with the "not knowing." We believe the person is ignoring us because we're not interesting to them. The not knowing is what is most difficult for us. So our mind creates a story with a catastrophic and unhappy ending.

There is risk in checking the story with the person. That would be courageous, the kind of work that could liberate us from the shackles of our own minds. If we continue to be fearful, through the manufacture and belief of the stories we tell ourselves and others, we will create an illusion for and about ourselves. And this illusion will keep us as victims of circumstance. It is only by facing our fears that we can rid ourselves of this illusion, unearth our inner self, and truly find freedom.

Making choices

Life is about choice. We have many choices to make; they occur daily. Not choosing is even a choice. Our resistance to seeing that we always have a choice is what creates much of the pain in our lives. We experience the pain as a state of "victimhood" in which things are "done to us." We're so afraid of this pain and do anything we can to avoid it. And in this avoidance, this running away, we create more pain.

Again, we get in our own way. Our true power as human beings is buried beneath the pain. Our unwillingness to explore, to experience, and to take ownership of how we have created the pain imprisons us. We need to be willing to understand this and to focus on what we really want. No more running away.

But admitting what we really want raises the possibility of new pain, of a new fear, because we're faced with the responsibility of bringing this state into being. We are completely accountable if we fail to do so. This fear further limits our ability to be self-aware. It limits our ability to move forward. Yet again, we are in our own way.

Love, marriage, divorce

There is a natural arc to all relationships: a beginning, a middle, and an end. We're lousy at the end for many reasons; primarily because we don't accept change well and don't deal with the ultimate change — death — well. The collapse of a relationship parallels death — the death of the dream that was the relationship — and the emotions are those of loss. In this state of turmoil, we have no closure; we're in a state of incompletion.

It is critical for us to move through our feelings at the conclusion of a relationship; otherwise we will have to face them later in life. These unresolved issues will hold us back and preoccupy our thoughts and as a consequence become the filter through which we skew our ability to experience new relationships.

You see, once upon a time there was the fairy tale of love and marriage. Divorce came along as a consequence of the inequities of the traditional relationship. Now we have inherited divorce. Love, marriage, and divorce — this is the new pattern in our culture. The Relationship Revolution calls us to take divorce off the table. We need to renew the understanding of what the commitment of a marriage really means. Removing divorce from that equation, refusing ourselves that easy way out, will enable us to focus on the relationship, on ourselves, and on each other. Not for a minute am I suggesting that we submit ourselves to a marriage of misery. What I am calling for is that we actually commit to co-creating a relationship that works for both parties, where each person feels good about the relationship.

In my experience, most of us married people are unwilling to enter the transformational fire that allows us to emerge into true adulthood. But we cannot truly join the other in the sacredness of marriage without going through this refining process — no exceptions. We need to be in that mental realm, that place where we can say to ourselves, without judgment, *my life is good.*

A crucible is a vessel with the capacity to hold molten metal. It's hot in there. When iron is heated to melting point, all the impurities are burned off. Relationship is a crucible that refines our impurities. The moment we judge that we should be in some other place in life, we completely close off the ability to learn from where we are. We miss not only the point but also a monumental opportunity. We are, yet again, in our own way.

We cannot change what has happened in our life. We can change how we perceive it. It really is about changing our thoughts about our past, about changing our mind. Life is perception, which is why others don't see the world or events in that world the same way we do. It doesn't mean that either person in the relationship is right or wrong; it just means that what each perceives is different, based on different experiences.

Failure — and recovery

The Relationship Revolution also requires us to redefine what failure means. We need to be able to fail and recover gloriously rather than being so hard on ourselves for our humanness. Our judgment that there are good experiences and bad experiences is arrogant — as if we know the difference between a good experience and a bad one! I have learned the most about myself and what matters from the painful experiences of my life. These experiences are therefore the most important to me. We need the contrast inherent in our experiences to know the difference between what is healing and what is destructive in relationship.

Culturally we are in the midst of a positive-thinking movement. We're supposed to think only positive thoughts, hang with positive people, and have positive experiences. A battery has a positive and negative charge; otherwise it wouldn't generate power. Truth is like that. We need the contrast of experiences to know what we want. My father's emotional unavailability was painful to me as a child and could be viewed as a negative experience. Today I can see it as a gift because it has taught me the value of being emotionally available. To judge any experience as negative or a failure is a subtle form of blame, and we lose the lesson that's available to us for our evolution.

To create movement in your life, answer the
following question:

What would you have to resolve within
yourself in order for your relationship to
operate with a sense of ease?

To gain a deeper understanding, please go to
relationshipexcellence.com to post your thoughts
and read responses from others who are also
committed to creating relationship excellence.

2

Relationship Excellence
You can't mend the fence while you're sitting on it

THERE ARE THREE DISTINCT PARTS to a relationship. There is the you, there is the me, and finally there is the thing we co-create, the relationship. The relationship, or the third entity as it is sometimes called, is the part we need to focus on, not the actual people in the relationship. Once we move away from you and me, we can get clear about what the relationship needs in order for us to thrive. We can achieve relationship excellence.

Loving the relationship

What would happen if we learned to love the experience of being in the relationship more than the other person in that relationship?

A relationship is the result of what both people contribute to it. One person alone cannot create it. One person can, however, have a huge impact on and set the tone for this third entity. The relationship is very much a culmination of the two individualities and the consequent union of these two individualities, complete with all their nuances and intentions.

Relationship is like a big pot of soup. Each individual brings different ingredients to the soup. The intermingling of those ingredients is what gives it its flavor. Bitter vegetables will result in a bitter-flavored soup. Vegetables that complement one other, bringing out one another's unique flavoring, will result in a full-bodied, better-tasting soup. It is incumbent on us to be conscious of the ingredients that we're contributing to relationship — and of the overall effect of those ingredients on the relationship. Being in relationship calls us to notice, at every point, our impact on the relationship and to take responsibility for and adjust ourselves in accordance with our intentions for the relationship.

And just as it takes two people to make a relationship work, so it takes two to destroy it. Except for extraordinary circumstances in which pathological abuse is involved, both members of a relationship are equally responsible for the ending of the relationship — and for the way it ends. The emotions, thoughts, and very often blame make it difficult for the members of a relationship to see the situation objectively. As Einstein said, "You cannot solve a problem from the same consciousness that created it." Einstein refers to the necessity of self-consciousness and self-awareness. Both of these can be learned by seeing the relationship as a vehicle for personal growth. There is no better way to learn about ourselves than in a close, intimate relationship.

The strategy of blame and faultfinding, in which the focus is placed on one person as bearing responsibility for the relationship's failure, is therefore flawed. Unfortunately, finding blame is common in most relationships. The blame strategy contradicts the fundamentals of a relationship: understanding our individual roles and being cognizant, conscious, and clear in seeing and understanding ourselves and our contribution.

The blame strategy is the very reason the relationship is in peril in the first place. All of this blame is further exacerbated when the relationship finally ends. How we end a relationship is as critical as how we begin it. Endings are a place where many of us are re-wounded, a place where we must have a deliberate, conscious intention to honor the other person as well as ourselves. When this doesn't happen, the re-wounding is taken into our subsequent relationships, inevitably causing them injury. It isn't a crime when people discover that they don't want the same thing as each other. It's a crime when they won't let go, insisting that the other has to want what they want.

I once worked with a couple who had six children. The couple were not married, but the woman had devoted herself to the man as if they were, even legally changing her last name to his. She clearly picked him and gave him six sons. He couldn't contemplate marrying her because he had been so wounded by a previous divorce. His wounds were both emotional and financial, because his ex-wife "took half the assets" from their short marriage. Now, in his new relationship, he lost himself in his work, justifying his workaholism with the necessity of supporting the family. She complained that he wasn't available to her. She overspent on things they didn't need as a coping mechanism for her pain and to force him to pay attention to her. This caused his financial wound to resurface. Their relationship fragmented, with serious consequences to them and their children. In addition, both of them had unconscious family of origin issues at play in the relationship.

When a relationship is no longer joyful and the parties involved seem unable or unwilling to shift from their state of pain, outside assistance is needed. Asking for help is an intelligent and responsible move. It is not a sign of weakness. Many men believe counseling is for the weak. But if they broke their arm, wouldn't they seek professional attention? They need to develop the same attitude when it comes to fragmented relationships. We need to be willing to love the relationship enough to do whatever it takes to shift our own state.

Most people, however — whether through shame, embarrassment, or even fear — wait too long before seeking a catalyst to change the direction of their relationship. Simply put, the sooner we attend to the pain in the relationship, the greater the degree of success we'll have in healing its wounds.

To create movement in your life, answer the following question:

What emotional baggage from your family of origin is blocking you in your current relationship?

To gain a deeper understanding, please go to relationshipexcellence.com to post your thoughts and read responses from others who are also committed to creating relationship excellence.

The bigger picture

People often report that their relationship has problems. But in reality, relationships don't have problems; people bring their wounds and their problems into the relationship and these in turn have an impact on that relationship. Problems are simply an invitation to look at ourselves, to look at the bigger picture of what is happening. If we took our resistance as an invitation to figure out what we're resisting, what we're being called to learn about ourselves, we might well feel gratitude for ourselves and experience a new sense of freedom.

I continually revisit this constant in relationship: this notion that the participants in the relationship dictate not only what they are contributing to that relationship, but also the health of the relationship itself. The relationship itself is a vehicle, if you will, for holding, respecting, and honoring each other's unique contributions. This understanding — this consciousness — is the way through the hardships of any relationship. Each person must take responsibility for the parts they bring to the relationship and their impact on the relationship. They must also take responsibility for the parts they don't bring. As Gandhi said, "Be the change that you wish to see in the world."

Our relationship gives us an opportunity to heal the wounds we have brought into it from our past. The sun of love will naturally bring these wounds to light. Instead of seeing their emergence as a signal to run, we need only apply the love of the relationship to the healing of the relationship. We are continually re-wounded in a relationship when we feel judged either by others or ourselves. When we judge our partner, we are working against them and are responsible for the impact this has on the relationship.

What would need to change in us so compassion and curiosity, rather than judgments, are brought to the fore? We must remember that both parties are equally and one hundred percent responsible for the state and nurture of the relationship and how it is attended to.

A relationship is an opportunity for learning and having fun together — and for healing old wounds that each sustained before knowing the other. Imagine developing that level of consciousness *through* our relationship and constantly applying it *to* our relationship. We would automatically become aware of our own judgments and fears while creating the safety to grow together through curiosity and openness.

> To create movement in your life, answer the following question:
>
> How can you invite your partner to join you in co-creating relationship excellence when they don't feel ready to do so?
>
> To gain a deeper understanding, please go to relationshipexcellence.com to post your thoughts and read responses from others who are also committed to creating relationship excellence.

Asking for help

When couples ask for help, they usually seek it using one of three different strategies — or, to put it more precisely, their relationships do.

Some couples want the pain to go away and things to go back to the way they were. This is impossible because life is constantly changing: It is either growing and evolving or decaying and dying. This desire for things to go back to the way they were before, when we first met, before the affair, or before the children, whatever the scenario may be, is impossible to attain. There simply is no going back. Life changes us, situations change us, and people's actions change us. We are designed to move forward in our lives. Through the passage of time, we inevitably discover more about ourselves, and this change is constant. This band-aid approach, this instant-pain-relief strategy, may be effective, in the short term. But it fails, in the long term, because it simply masks the true nature of the hardships.

When dealing with couples taking this strategy, I usually ask, "Would you rather have, one sharp pain or a dull ache for the rest of your life?" Most people don't want either. Most believe that pain, of any kind or of any intensity, is horrible and unimaginable and must be avoided at all cost. This pain-avoidance, pleasure-seeking predisposition is counterproductive. Pain is our best teacher; it waves a red flag to grab our attention. The quick-fix strategy is equivalent to an excursion to the mall or a tall gin and tonic when we're feeling down — ways to stall reality. Suppress any pain in a relationship and it will resurface. Furthermore, the means of suppression may create even more significant pain, such as debt, alcoholism, resentment, and depression.

Other couples take the tack of indicating that there is an "identified patient" in the relationship — the other person, who is in need of "fixing." A relationship in this state has little hope of flourishing. Nobody enjoys being blamed, and a relationship based on blame or full of blame simply results in contempt, frustration, and anger.

Our approach to life is shot through with blame. No matter what the problem, we believe that someone needs to be identified as the problem, blamed, and held accountable; only then can we know what to do. This belief blinds us to the fact that both are responsible for the state of the relationship. If we're to thrive in relationship, we have to eliminate blame completely. The mere act of laying blame robs us of the opportunity to learn what we need to in order to find a resolution. Once we're in the blame game, we're always in the blame game.

A relationship in which one person needs fixing will soon be broken. One or both will feel so wounded that they will leave the relationship emotionally. Again, until the two players see the relationship as a dance that must be finely crafted, with both working on their own steps to the same tune, getting back to relational health is impossible. The relationship will become lifeless and end badly.

Other couples — and unfortunately they are a minority — take the third strategy, one that helps relationships not only survive but thrive. Using this strategy, couples, as individuals, are willing to take the responsibility for doing whatever it takes to make the relationship work. They relinquish blame for the other and themselves. They become absolutely curious about how their relationship got where it is. This allows the magic and mystery of relationship to unfold. This strategy gives each person has the opportunity to determine what they really want to change about themselves in order to contribute more to the relationship. These couples get to see the impact of those changes on the relationship, which helps them continue to discover how best to support each other.

A subtle collusion often develops within a relationship. For example, "I won't challenge you about the money you spend on the credit card and you don't get to challenge me on my drinking." Couples operating on the basis of collusion rarely tell the truth in front of each other in couples counseling. The process cannot be successful because the "withhold" is in the way. A relationship cannot heal until the whole truth is revealed.

I always conduct an interview with each person separately before counseling them together. This helps them to establish and reveal the truth. I refuse to be the holder of secrets; my refusal helps me encourage clients to reveal their complete truth to each other.

I recall a client who had come to me because he was having an affair and was fairly certain that he wanted to end his marriage. At one point in his coaching he realized that he needed to tell his wife the truth. She was extremely upset, not so much because his revelation meant the end of the marriage, but because she had been having an affair for several years and her husband hadn't noticed or challenged her on her emotional absence from the relationship.

Unfortunately most couples only flirt with the idea of getting support for their relationship. At the first sign of relief from the tension they're feeling, they conclude that there's no need to continue the process. Rather than seeing the process as an ongoing one of deeper discovery, their response is, "Oh well, we're through that now."

To create movement in your life, answer the
following question:

What, from your perspective, is the collusion
at play in your relationship that is causing
both of you to be less than your best?

To gain a deeper understanding, please go to
relationshipexcellence.com to post your thoughts
and read responses from others who are also
committed to creating relationship excellence.

A commitment to growth

By the time a couple realizes that they need to take this
third strategy, they need to revise their understanding
of what they long to co-create in their relationship. This
is a process of re-discovery, personal ownership, and
accountability through growth. Couples discover this process to be one of individually and collectively choosing
how they want to live their lives. Because they are truly
committed to relationship, they are willing to do whatever it takes to achieve that desired outcome, which likely
includes getting support and learning a new skill set. True
commitment demands each gain the discipline to do
whatever it takes to achieve their goal.

Think about this in terms of exercise. If we commit
to running a marathon and don't understand that our

exercise routine must be changed, that we need to learn new skills, get support, and re-groove our behavior, we will inevitably fail, suffering additional pain. In relationship, making new commitments — and keeping them — requires us to change our behavior patterns. The adage "judge me for my actions and not my words" applies here.

Most people, when they commit to something, continue to do what it is they know how to do, which likely means the commitment fails. Making a commitment involves moving to a higher plane of action and consciousness. It may even require us to grow into a new experience. Commitment involves us fully as part of a relationship. When two people in a relationship have moved to this plane, they discover that there really is no place for divorce: The commitment demands that both stay open to supporting the relationship and to co-creating what is needed for the relationship to thrive. The relationship really is much bigger than either individual.

Commitment versus attachment

It is important, however, to distinguish between commitment and attachment. Do you know the difference? Let's draw on a weight-loss analogy. If I am committed to losing weight and having a healthy body, that commitment is mine; only I can do it. True, I may enlist a personal trainer or nutritionist to support me in reaching my goal, and asking for and receiving support is in fact critical to attaining my desired outcomes. But ultimately I am the one who has to exercise. I am the one who has to make wise food choices that will help support my commitment. The power resides within me.

In contrast, when I become attached to an outcome, it always involves another person. If I tell you not to bring ice cream or junk food into the house because I am committed to losing weight, I have placed the power of my outcome on you. My success depends on the way I want you to behave.

Attachment is detrimental to the end goal. It brings drama, misery, and chaos into relationship. It is a form of control that is rooted in fear: the fear that we cannot do it by ourselves, that we need others to "do it for us."

Whether we are attached to people seeing us a particular way or to others behaving a certain way, we need to see any attachment for what it is. Operating with attachment is draining. It exhausts the relationship. The classic sign of attachment is one partner kicking the other under the table during a meal with friends to stop them from saying or doing something. This is an opportunity to look within.

The ceremony of marriage is perhaps the most defining moment of commitment. Yet it would be interesting to explore and understand what we have really been committing to over the centuries. Could it be that the very fundamentals are contributing to the ever-increasing divorce rate? Quite possibly. The things we commit to at the beginning of marriage are ridiculous. Why? Because at the time of marriage we have no idea what they truly mean. And we have no understanding of the transformational process we must undergo for the relationship to thrive. A *vow* is defined as *a solemn promise to perform a certain act, carry out an activity, or behave in a given way*. But when we take the marriage vow, we speak it relative to the conditions of the time: romantic love, idealism, and usually a lack of experience.

It bears repeating: We need to understand that being in a relationship requires us to pass through a transformational fire that will burn off the residues of our beleaguered past. True commitment is the container in which the stuff of the relationship can be worked through. This can happen only when two people are committed to staying in the tension with the understanding that they are there to serve not themselves but the relationship and its transformation. Rather than become complacent in our vows, we need to be willing and able to feel and stay with the tension, uncertainty, and even turmoil. We squirm when we're in this place, which is good, because it means we're living on our edge, and that is where we are truly alive.

Commitment and relationship excellence

There are actually very few things in relationship we can truly commit to and fully carry out with success. Traditionally we commit to outcomes like staying together forever or loving each other unconditionally. We don't realize till later that this is actually a challenging process of understanding that never stops. We can commit only to the

process. It is not possible for us to commit to the outcome. This process includes:

- exploring and revealing our truth in a loving
  way
- taking responsibility for all of our feelings and
  eliminating blame
- keeping and holding the agreements we make
  as sacred
- getting serious and lightening up through play
  and gratitude.

These commitments are the underpinning of relationship
excellence.

> To create movement in your life, answer the
> following question:
>
> How would you describe the dance of your
> relationship? Be sure to include your steps as
> well as your partner's (from your perspective).
>
> To gain a deeper understanding, please go to
> relationshipexcellence.com to post your thoughts
> and read responses from others who are also
> committed to creating relationship excellence.

3

The Purpose of Relationship
The pain of being stuck can get you past the fear of change

UNTIL WE'RE WILLING TO MAKE peace with our parents —
accepting who they are in the world and who they have
been — we will continue to be haunted by our unresolved issues with them. Whether we realize it or not, we
use our present primary relationships to resolve our past
primary relationships. If we had issues with our parents'
authority, we will paste these issues on the authority figures
in our lives today. If we weren't loved the way we wanted
to be loved by a parent, we will be needy in our romantic
relationships. If we grew up with critical or emotionally
absent parents, our oversensitive antennae will pick up
the slightest signal of criticism or disconnection.

Unless we recognize the pattern and beliefs we hold
within ourselves, courtesy of our beliefs from our parents
and our family of origin, we will miss out on creating and
enjoying a wonderful dance, together. A major purpose
of relationship is to heal the wounds that we bring with

us to relationship. We are challenged in our capacity to de-role our parents because at base we need to replace their parenting of us with our parenting of ourselves. Our parents may have a hard time relinquishing their firm grip on our lives — we may have had to wrestle it from them. We need to have compassion for our parents, who to varying degrees have spent a large portion of their lives caring for and raising us.

As we face the rules and structures that they have set up for us, we may come to the conclusion that many of them no longer work for us. Our evolution may be painful for our parents to handle. It is critical, as we grow and evolve, that we represent to them that these changes are about us, not them. This will help us refrain from what often happens when children evolve, from blaming our parents for their wrongdoings and wounding them in the process.

For many people the act of bringing up their own children reinforces pain from their own childhood, pain that needs to be healed or it will inadvertently be passed on. However, parenting can also cause them to develop understanding and deep compassion for their parents along with gratitude for the privilege and responsibility that are now theirs.

I always ask people to describe for me the real meaning of relationship. It is incumbent on me to establish what people make words mean, because there's a difference between what the words themselves mean and the personal meaning people overlay on them. Disagreements happen when we think we are talking about the same meaning.

I ask, "What does a relationship mean to you?" and receive such answers as having fun together, sharing, companionship, watching movies, creating family, connecting with friends, and weekends away. All these responses are about doing things, or what I call *recreation* as opposed to *relationship*.

I see relationship as being aware of or understanding another's way of being. Let's look at this more closely. To *become aware of* or *understand* means to observe a person and how they interact in their world. We gain substantial information from being with another in a doing capacity — when we're sharing in an activity. We need to cultivate an observer's mind, gathering information through a sense of curiosity about the other as well as ourselves. Only then can we determine what the dance between us really looks like.

The instrument of the mind that destroys this awareness is judgment. When we judge we automatically place people, places, and things in boxes. The boxes of good or bad, of right or wrong, of reasonable or unreasonable all separate us from gaining an understanding or being aware of another's way of being. We close down to the learning as we bump up against our own childhood training about what it means to be in relationship.

We each come to relationship with our own preconceptions of how relationships are supposed to be. We are trained to be in relationship through our experiences of

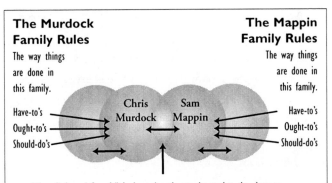

The Murdock Family Rules

The way things are done in this family.

Have-to's
Ought-to's
Should-do's

The Mappin Family Rules

The way things are done in this family.

Have-to's
Ought-to's
Should-do's

Chris Murdock   Sam Mappin

When Chris and Sam fall in love, they dream about what they long to co-create. This is all the stuff that they make up about what is important to them.

This relationship will at some point be dominated by the rules that each person brings from their family of origin. These are the ways things "have to be" and they will have a push-pull effect on the relationship.

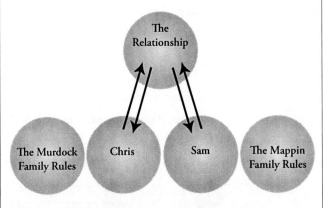

The Relationship

The Murdock Family Rules   Chris   Sam   The Mappin Family Rules

The Relationship Revolution

The Relationship Revolution calls on each of the individuals to focus their attention on supporting the relationship as a separate entity from themselves.

The notion is: How can I serve the relationship?

Healthy boundaries are maintained between the rules from our own families of origin and the rules that we co-create for our own relationship.

growing up in our families. Every family operates within a system that includes the dynamic each parent has received from *their* family of origin. Then there is the dynamic that our parents have formed with each other. There is also the dynamic that our parents have with each of their siblings and between us and our siblings.

This is a complex clash of family systems that need to be sorted out so we can see the connections between parents and their families, between parents and siblings. (Go to relationshipexcellence.com to download your free Family of Origin Rules Chart. This will support you in getting clear on your family system rules.)

On the basis of our family systems we determine that things need to be a particular way — or, out of reaction to the way we were brought up, that they need to be different. We are always working, either consciously or unconsciously, in reaction to or in alignment with the training we have inherited from our family system.

It's no wonder then that when two people come together and start a relationship, each is impacted by the beliefs and values that were instilled in them from their early years in their own families. Most of us enjoy and want to perpetuate within our current relationship certain aspects of our family system. Most of us also wish to obliterate certain other aspects from our memory, let alone our current relationship.

One thing I enjoy, in reaction to my family system, is the custom of taking the time to sit at a table nicely set with tablecloth, plates, and cutlery when we eat together. I want no part of the way anger was expressed in my family, with meals served functionally and the table a field of battle.

As a result of our family system, we will have fixed perspectives on "the right way" to do certain things. Whether it is education, saving, spending, bedtime routines, or the way a home is decorated and by whom, the list is endless. We are challenged in relationship when we join with a partner who has just as much invested in their "right way" as we do.

Let the clashes begin!

How we deal with this level of conflict is what sets the tone for the evolution of the relationship.

Giving birth to your self

Growing up, then, is a process of maturing in which we examine and dispel the stories about ourselves that we have created from childhood on. Some of the stories may have been fed to us. We may have been told we were the one with brains while our sibling was the beautiful one. Or we were stupid or silly. Growing up requires that we examine the truth about those experiences and the stories we made up about them, creating freedom for ourselves in the process.

This evolutionary process is essentially one of giving birth to ourselves. It requires courage and discipline. Birth is messy. It is not packaged in a neat little box. It is the process of getting to the deepest truth of who we are. We are all divine beings with choice.

The very essence of relationship is this process of healing the wounds we carry from our family of origin. At our core, we all want the same thing. Like humans throughout time and the world over, we want to share experiences, emotions, and events, uniting with others in our likeness. We have all experienced disappointment, hurt, loss, betrayal, abandonment, joy, and bliss. The list is endless, yet the common element among the items is this: the desire to share the same experiential bond of the things on this list, to share our humanness, to recognize that though we are each unique, we are all very much the same.

We have to come to terms with the reality that as human beings we make mistakes and screw up. We aren't honest and loyal all the time. This is part of our uniqueness and part of our humanness. We make mistakes. Being in relationship requires us, therefore, to live with an open heart. We must be receptive to that idea of innate flaw, all the while accepting that we always have choice: the opportunity to evolve and reach relationship excellence.

We may not realize it, but we are always at choice. We don't have to accept everything that comes our way. We get to decide whether we live with an open heart or a bruised heart. Some people have been so bruised that they have decided to close their heart. It actually isn't possible for us to truly close our heart, but we can create for ourselves a slow death in the trying: a sad and lonely life. We may close our hearts because we have decided we don't want to get hurt in relationship, but then we will experience limited enjoyment and freedom in relationship. We need to accept that we will get hurt in relationship because we will at times create misunderstandings. How we resolve the misunderstandings — that is what brings back the joy.

We are a pair-bonding species, plain and simple. We have a deep longing for companionship and connection. For proof we need only look at how we get married and divorced and then promptly return to relationship again. In fact, this longing to connect is so deep, some of us find ourselves in another relationship long before the original one has been completed. And we unconsciously follow the same patterns as before, eventually finding ourselves stuck in an all-too-familiar place.

Someone said we spend our childhood surviving the ordeal of growing up only to spend our adulthood trying to get over it. We're inevitably wounded in the process of navigating childhood. We all carry wounds from our upbringing.

My life changed radically when I chose to see all the people around me as having been wounded in some way or another. This perspective allows me to see others and myself as fully human and fallible.

A wound can originate from an innocent statement, such as "You're lazy," or a more blatant one, such as "You were an accident." To varying degrees, part of our behavior is dictated by our wounds, both conscious and unconscious. I can now make the distinction between who a person is at their core and their behavior. I don't have to take their behavior personally. While I am responsible for my own behavior, I can be curious about what wounds may be driving my own actions.

We react in one of two ways in dealing with our childhood wounds. One is to deny reality. Some of us not only fail to recognize our own wounds but also believe ourselves to have had a charmed upbringing. The other is to wallow in reality: to be so immersed in our wounds that we experience them as all encompassing in the here and now. We recall them with a sense of pride, wearing them almost as a badge of honor.

Greg, a man I once coached, took the denial route. He grew up poor in the north of Canada. And I mean poor. His family never knew where their next meal was coming from. His dad was an alcoholic and drank away what little money he earned. As an adolescent, Greg acted out his anger by becoming a bully. His face bore the marks of the fights he picked, though he maintained with pride that he won most of them.

Today, Greg is financially successful. He happily pays for many of his family members to have a better life. He's still a bully, however. Business is now his playground, and lawyers are now his fists. After his marriage failed, he committed himself to providing his ex-wife with a generous income but refused to settle financially with her. Why? Because he didn't want to reveal his net worth to her lawyers. He actually spent several hundred thousand dollars every year to hide his worth.

Not surprisingly, Greg's behavior got in the way of a

deep relationship with the new woman in his life. He was unwilling to look at and take responsibility for how his childhood wound was still running his life through his need to create certainty today. He was a prisoner of his own making, blinded by his own success.

A woman I worked with who was raped as a teenager took the other route. She told everyone she met about the traumatic event. She constantly replayed it, making it the central part of her identity and re-traumatizing herself in the process. Her perspective was getting in her way, blocking her from creating the relationship she wanted. It caused her to typecast all men as potential rapists. No man was safe. She had successfully created herself as the perpetual victim.

Like both of these people, we all carry emotional scars from our past. Some are clearly visible for all to see, and some are hidden, buried deep within. Either way, the wounds that caused these scars have a tremendous effect on our behavior patterns in adulthood. They dictate how we function individually and within society. To grow, we must be curious about and intensely conscious of their effect. This is the only way to fully understand why we behave the way we do and to fully grasp how we are at choice to change.

The unconscious relationship

The difference between a wound and a scar is that a wound has the potential to be re-opened. Only when we have worked through the pain of our wounding and come to accept the situations that created them can we let go and let them heal. When we're not conscious of how our wounds are contributing to and shaping our lives, they are easily reopened. When we're living what I call the unconscious relationship, we don't know where our feelings end and those of others begin. As a result, we either end up feeling responsible for everything that goes on in the relationship or for none of it. We're triggered into old hurts by the very people we love, often ending up feeling more hurt. Emotionally overwhelmed, we act out of our own wounds. We may become controlling or accusatory; we may withdraw or punish the other or ourselves.

The irony is that we are triggered not only by the things others do or say but just as likely by the things they don't do or say. Either way, the trigger is ours to work through. In an exchange with a partner who resorts to nagging, we might say, "My mother used to nag me; I can't stand it when you do that." This trigger is an opportunity to remember the powerlessness we felt as a child and grow through the experience as an adult. When we take responsibility for the feeling in the here and now, we can teach our partner a way to share information so it will be heard.

Remember, we teach others how to treat us. Just because we love each other is no guarantee that we will communicate effectively with each other. When we're committed to the relationship, we are willing to modify our communication so we both feel good about the outcome.

Our unwillingness to take responsibility for our triggers will serve to deepen our wounds, leaving us feeling more hurt than healed in the relationship, eventually leading to the relationship's demise. Faced with enough of this pain, we opt out of relationships altogether, not wanting to get hurt anymore. Or, when we do meet someone, we present them with a bill for payment: a list of all the past hurts and transgressions we have experienced at the hands of others, which we feel they must make up to us.

I worked with a man who had come to Canada as a teenager, losing contact with many of his friends from the old country. A full twenty-five years later he received an e-mail from a good friend who had also moved away. She had gone to Greece when he had left for Canada. The e-mail was a request to see if he was the man she had gone to college with. He was and in her second e-mail she included many photos from their friendship together. In those days it took a long time for photographs to load onscreen. This man told me that the first picture to load was of the two of them at an amusement park; it brought back fond memories, he said. The next photo was of the two of them standing with his first girlfriend. All of his feelings about that relationship filled his soul as the picture filled the screen.

At the tender age of seventeen he had caught her cheating with his best friend. He had walked away from the relationship, burying his feelings of betrayal, anger, and hurt and deciding never to let anyone ever hurt him that much again. As he saw this photograph he realized the enormity of never having dealt with those feelings: that he had unconsciously left every relationship he had been in since. This came to him just as he was preparing to exit his current relationship. He chose instead to face his re-wounding, break the pattern of his script, and stay and work things out.

The way many people function in relationship demonstrates that they haven't grown up and definitely haven't left home. They are still under the spell of their "familiar" experience and are therefore destined to re-experience it.

Growing up and leaving home requires a willingness to become conscious of the wounds and stories controlling and influencing our behavior: to challenge the beliefs and structures we have lived with and discover whether they really are true and real. Such an exploration, like leaving home for the first time, is in itself liberating. But liberation can be frightening. Having held ourselves captive within a structure for so many years, we are reluctant to leave it.

Creating stories

Stories are the scripts and decisions implicit or explicit in our lives that we invent out of our childhood wounds and family rules. We act them out over and over again. We are able to break the hold they have one us only once we come to see them for the illusion that they are. I recall at age nine being asked to paint a forest. "Owen, don't you know that trees aren't blue, they're green?" my art teacher said to me. My favorite trees are blue spruce, so that's what I painted. I decided in that moment that I wasn't creative and was no good at art. It wasn't till thirty years later that I was able to see and experience how creative I truly am.

A friend of mine went home for Christmas every year until she was forty. She resented the four-hour drive to her parents' house, the quick stay over, then the five-hour drive to her in-laws. The ordeal took the joy out of Christmas for her. Her story was that everyone in the family simply had to attend. Finally she decided to break with tradition and create her own Christmas experience in her own home. When she mustered up the courage to tell her parents, she was surprised by how receptive and encouraging they were.

I was hit as a child. While this was perhaps normal back then, today it would fall within the parameters of child abuse. At around the age of five, I made a decision. At the time it was the only reasonable decision I could make, because it helped me make sense of what was happening to me. I decided I was bad. I set about collecting and creating evidence to prove the truth of my story.

Then, in 1973, when I left home on my sixteenth birthday to attend college, I decided, *Enough with being bad and miserable; I'm going to be joyful.* So I became Mr. Happy, making the best of every situation. I used my exit from home to do a complete one-eighty, viewing even the most unpleasant of things with a smile.

My life was amazing. I was learning, I was passionate about things, I had a job, money, and a social life. I rose to any occasion and made the best of it. Being Mr. Happy came at a cost, however. It required me to never say no to people and to continually manage and control situations to minimize conflict. A fellow student called me out on this, saying I wasn't being real, but for many years I didn't understand what he meant. I chose not to hang around him.

Ironically, my coping mechanism helped me become skillful at intervening. I did very well for myself in my career as a manager. I was a people person and became adept far beyond my years at handling difficult situations. I rose quickly through the ranks of my business. By the time I was in my mid-twenties, I was earning a six-figure income and had several hundred people reporting to me. I became a workaholic, exhausted more by the rigors of propping up my false identity than by my actual work. By this time my perfectionism was in full swing. I had to look as if I was perfect in order to gain approval and please people.

However, no matter how many accolades and acknowledgments I received, Mr. Happy never felt happy. I was always afraid someone would see through me like the young man in college: see that I wasn't real — that far from being happy, I was scared and felt like a fraud.

Suddenly I was looking my worst fear in the eye. What if I was truly bad? Was I truly happy? From that point on, I had to confront the fears I felt as a child and the decisions I had made as a result. Now, as an adult, I had to take a hard look at them and discover "my truth." What was actually true about me and my world? I was taking big steps, necessary ones if I was to grow up and be me.

The psychiatrist Carl Jung states that in the morning of life "all that really matters is that we gain quantity of experience" and that in the afternoon of life "we are searching for quality of experience." This has been proven true in my life. He says further — and this is of monumental importance — that "in the afternoon of life we [must] discover that everything we thought was true in the morning of life is in fact untrue." Jung counsels a radical shake-up, one that is disorienting initially but is crucial for understanding ourselves and making a successful transition into adulthood.

Sloughing off the skin of "being a bad kid," even though it wasn't true, was very painful for me. It required a conscious disconnect from my paradoxical effort of living out the story that I was bad and desperately trying to disprove it through forced happiness. I had to choose to rid myself of that persona and become the person I really was. The experience was at times terrifying and at times liberating. I also had to forgive myself for the pain I had inflicted on myself by living out this illusion.

Get serious and lighten up

We are supposed to be having a good time as we travel through life. If we aren't having fun, chances are we're being way too serious. When the fun has gone out of our relationship, all that is left is chores.

We need to ask ourselves: Why am I the way I am in the world? Am I headed in the direction that will lead me to my desired destination? Am I on the right path?

Most people I meet seem to be wandering aimlessly about. Or they're so serious, they're missing out on key moments of the journey.

If we lack a vision of where we're heading, the winds of time will dictate our course. We need to get serious and take charge of life, creating what it is we truly desire. And we need to lighten up and commit ourselves to having a good time; otherwise everything becomes a chore. Think of how children learn. Whether they're getting on the school bus or eating a snack, it is all play to them. We have lost our childlike sense of wonder and excitement about ourselves and the world. We need to reclaim and recapture that joy and innocence.

As an adolescent I judged my parents as having no dreams for themselves. It was only as I was writing my mother's eulogy, thirty years after I had left home, that I realized how untrue this was of her: that she not only had a powerful dream but also was committed to bringing it into reality. My mother was clear about her role. She wanted to prepare her children for the world, and to prepare us to fly without her.

Many people, including the minister, tried to talk me out of speaking at the funeral service. It will be too difficult, they said. You might break down. Worse, you might not be able to deliver it at all. (And what if my breakdown interrupted the process and delayed the next funeral? Can you imagine!) The importance of this task overrode any such fears, however. As I spoke, I knew in every fiber of my being that my mother had fulfilled her unwavering and unshakable commitment to preparing me for life. There are many things I could have and at times did criticize her for, but they faded into insignificance as I stood there at the end of her life, looking over her life's work — her children.

Know what you stand for

If we are going to enjoy the journey, we have to know where we're headed and what we would be prepared to die for. That may seem a bold statement, and it is true. If we know the answer to that question, we will know what we're willing to live for. It is that simple. We lose ourselves in relationships when we don't know what we stand for. We lose ourselves when our focus is out there on the other and not on the relationship and how we're serving it. Since our eyes are in the front of our heads, we spend most of our time looking at everyone else. What if we were willing to look within ourselves more often? What if we looked at our behavior and its impact on the relationship and our environment, instead of focusing on the behavior of others? We definitely would get a different picture of life, wouldn't we?

If we don't stand for something, we will fall for anything. When we know what matters to us, popular opinion won't sway us. Again, it is time we get serious about the journey and lighten up. Many of us fail to do this because we're attached to our need to be right. Instead of recognizing, cherishing, and enjoying the moments of our journey, we become preoccupied with this constant need. I marvel at the way people will argue over whether they showed up at exactly three p.m. or six minutes after. As we will see later in this book, if we are our word, then we will show up on time or at a minimum take responsibility for our lateness. This is about operating from excellence, not perfection. We need to get serious and lighten up!

One of the most powerful exercises I undertake from time to time is writing a eulogy to myself as I would like it to be written by others when I die. I am always curious why so many of my clients resist this assignment. Probably because the exercise scares up all the judgments they have about the way they are. They are forced to look at all their sorrows, all their regrets, their past behaviors and actions or inactions, everything. But this is precisely why the exercise is so powerful: It is precisely these self-judgments that are causing them to get in their own way. There is nothing like death to bring life fully before us. Such judgments will imprison us if they are not explored and discussed, truly limiting our ability to achieve success in relationships.

My mentor, Mrs. Lillie, used to tell me to go to as many funerals as possible. That way you will be faced with the truth about your life and you will live longer than your friends, she said. She went to a lot of funerals. She was just shy of one hundred and two when she died.

Years ago I took a three-hour drive each month to visit an inmate who was the son of a client. The inmate could-n't understand why I did it, but it seemed apparent to me: I wanted to be of service to this man and his family. A year into the visits, it dawned on me why I really was there. It was to discover what this man had to teach me.

He had used his time and intellect well in prison, becom-ing a keen observer of his own thoughts. He knew he wasn't his thoughts and that he was fully responsible for the choices and actions that came from his thoughts. For example, he knew that any drug he wanted from the street was readily available to him but turned them down because he wasn't willing to risk what he truly wanted: a chance at life with a different perspective. He was one of those rare creatures: a con who was actually rehabilitating himself during his time in prison. He was smart enough to realize that if he took on the prison guards' daily reinforcement that he was a criminal and that criminals end up in jail, he would have to return there.

This man's gift to me was his insight into the centrality of systems in our lives. He had honed his ability to see that he was part of a system. He realized that in order for that system to continue, he had to get sent back to it after he was released. If he didn't, he would impact the strength of the system.

We all take part in different systems with varying rules. Most of them are productive. Take the banking system, for example. So long as we have a mortgage, there are rules. Both the mortgagee and the mortgagor have to follow them. If we don't pay our monthly payment for three months, the bank has the right to seize our house. Some of them aren't. I worked in the educational system for many years and left because I felt that the rules of the system supported mediocrity as opposed to excellence. I set up my own system, which is my current business and life dream, in order to take a stand for excellence.

We are always at choice. We always get to look at the systems we're in and can choose to modify them or step outside them and create a new one.

If I drive my car over the speed limit, I may be fined. Whether I agree with it or not, so long as I get behind the wheel of the car, I am subscribing to the system and am subject to its rules. In a family system, the rules may be unspoken but the consequences of breaking them well known. If we sense or are told that we cannot challenge the way a system works, our only options are to rebel, surrender, or withdraw. The last two choices may be seen all too clearly in the sadness, complacency, and emotional remoteness of people who have abdicated their choice to fully participate in life.

> To create movement in your life, answer the
> following question:
>
> In what way do you punish your partner for
> not living up to your relationship rules?
>
> To gain a deeper understanding, please go to
> relationshipexcellence.com to post your thoughts
> and read responses from others who are also
> committed to creating relationship excellence.

The challenge

The challenge in relationship is to understand that both
of you have come from a system with different structures.
Often we can see dysfunctionality in our partner's family
while our own may be obscure to us. Few people like
having the faults of their family system pointed out to them.
In fact, we're likely to defend our family to the bitter end,
especially if the feedback we're receiving is true. The
attitude of what happens in this family stays in this
family is part of the structure of most family systems. The
deeper challenge lies in two different people from two
different systems joining and making a new and better
system of their own.

The diversity among family systems is broad. Some families focus on keeping the peace at any price, while others
hash out conflict and then get on with it. Most of us will

leave our family system thinking we will never do it that way when we're in charge. Often there are painful and unproductive parts to our family systems. This might include the keeping of secrets, collusion between a parent and a child, or the discarding of a person or part of the extended family because of an often unspoken conflict between others.

Until we're willing to consciously create a new system, we will either emulate our family system or reject it. We may do so consciously or not, but do it we will.

Why are people from diverse backgrounds so attracted to each other? I believe a bigger plan must be at work. In my work of coaching couples, I have always thought that no two people meet who aren't supposed to meet. This means the person we are with is perfect for us. Perfect in so far as they will bring to the table the exact experiences that will demand the growth and evolution necessary for us in the moment. The challenge is to accept that more is going on than is being spoken about. In the Relationship Revolution, we accept that everything going on in our life right now is perfect just as it is, for our highest good.

What matters is that we take the time, together, to create and understand the system we want to live in and choose to co-create. We always have the choice to use life events — whether trauma, death, loss of a career, ill health, or even infidelity — as opportunities for growth and evolution. Unless couples grow together, they will grow apart. It is important to remember that no two people are ever in the same place at exactly the same time. When

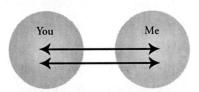

The Traditional Relationship

Individuals attempt to get their needs met by the other. This involves lots of:

- give and take
- or give and give
- or take and take

This relationship will be dominated by the rules that each person brings from their family of origin.

The notion is: What can I get from you and what will you give to me?

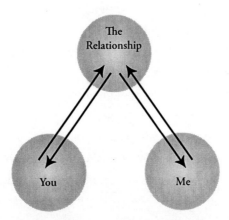

The Revolutionary Relationship

The Relationship Revolution calls on each of the individuals to focus their attention on supporting the relationship as a separate entity from themselves.

The notion is: How can I serve the relationship?

we're committed to growing together, we will need to develop an attitude of flexibility and patience. In fact, patience becomes the ultimate act of love.

So as our life unfolds and the mystery of life and attraction brings us together, we get to explore and experience our historic systems and ultimately choose the system we want.

To create movement in your life, answer the following question:

What rules from your family system are you stuck in, causing you to get in your own way?

To gain a deeper understanding, please go to relationshipexcellence.com to post your thoughts and read responses from others who are also committed to creating relationship excellence.

4

Words and Actions

It's not what you say that matters; it's what you do

PEOPLE COMMUNICATE A GREAT DEAL ABOUT themselves to us within the first fifteen minutes of our meeting them. Most of us miss this important opportunity to learn about the other, in many cases because of our own insecurities. We may hear people's words, but we interpret them against a backdrop of how we want to be seen. Consumed with whether or not they have the right opinion of us, we render their reality invisible.

The reality is that what another person thinks of us is none of our business. Their perception of us is skewed by their own experiences and their own interpretations. Our need to know that we are liked, approved of, and accepted arises from our insecurities, from our unrelenting need to be reassured that we are somehow enough. We make this our business because we're unclear about who we are and what we stand for in the world. This behavior is an example of how, once again, we are in our own way. Let me be clear: I'm not saying that we shouldn't care what others think of us. I'm saying that we need to be conscious that we impact others and therefore must be deliberate and conscious of that impact by being ourselves. Our wanting to be seen a particular way, or our attempt to manipulate people's views of us, by being protective and guarded and perhaps not truthful, is the very mechanism by which people incorrectly judge us. If, in contrast, we know ourselves well and communicate openly and authentically, we are tackling the issue on two fronts. First, we eliminate our self-doubt and thus are able to truly hear the other person. Second, we never have to question how we're being interpreted, because we have been honest and upfront in the way we have presented ourselves.

Most of us love to people watch because it gives us an opportunity to judge others, and judging others offers us a reprieve, however brief, from our own false self-assessment. We categorize ourselves as *better than* or *less than* when we compare ourselves with others. The better-than comparisons offer us a sense of superiority and pride. Though these judgments are false and short-lived, they are effective in making us feel good for the moment. The less-than comparisons breed self-doubt and resentment. If I think I am better than you, why should I talk to you? If I think I am less than you, why should you come and talk to me? Either way, I present myself as unapproachable. Better than and less than are boxes we put ourselves and others in. And being in a box is seen as a way of staying safe and protecting ourselves from others. The result is that we are stuck in a lonely place from which we cannot connect to another in relationship.

Life sentences

However, we cannot tamp down forever our longing to connect with another. We are a species that craves companionship and connection. When we join with another, we create a unique opportunity for self-introspection. This brings us to an edge: an awareness of the stories we have created.

What begins as stories in our life are acted out as models of behavior, and if they are allowed to continue unchallenged, they run our lives. Earlier we discussed how we all create stories about ourselves, especially during childhood but also into adulthood: stories by which we choose to live our lives. The awareness of these stories, and the conscious understanding of them, particularly when we're about to enter a relationship, together make up the choice point — the point at which we choose to continue on the path of disconnection and loneliness or take a new path of honesty, growth, and happiness.

These stories begin as sentences or phrases: "I am unlovable," "I am not enough," "I am not good enough." If allowed to continue, these judgments banish us to a life of isolation.

For many years, I defined myself with the sentence, "I am too much for others." When I spoke my truth and people became upset, I would challenge them, attempting to hold them to account. Naturally they became upset with me. I used their feedback to reinforce my story as fact. Being in this prison drastically affected my ability to connect fully with others.

How does this work? What we see in the world depends mainly on what we look for, so we gather the evidence and justification that supports our story. In fact, we defend these self-created stories about others and ourselves, often to our last breath.

To create a breakthrough and escape the oppressive bonds of these stories, we must first have breakdown. But breaking down is perhaps the hardest thing to accomplish. We are wound so tight, doing whatever it takes to hold things together. We are hyper-focused on filling the cracks that appear in the story of our life, hoping no one will notice. Our biggest fear is breaking down. We cannot allow ourselves the complete vulnerability that comes with such surrender, because our story and our identity, our false self, would come crumbling down. We would have to face the illusion of the identity we have been living through. The challenge is facing who we would be in that moment without the identity that we have portrayed. There's great beauty in this opportunity, because at this point we can finally become who we have always been: our true and natural self.

To create movement in your life, answer the following question:

What "life sentence" has banished you from fully living your life and relationship?

To gain a deeper understanding, please go to relationshipexcellence.com to post your thoughts and read responses from others who are also committed to creating relationship excellence.

Surrendering the story is essential. It creates the moment of clarity in which we learn about ourselves. We need to be curious about and observe our behavior. This can happen only when we slow down. Here's a truism that is true: The speed of life today is not conducive to self-awareness and connection. We need everything *now*: high-speed Internet, instant messaging, fast food, fast cars, and, yes, even speed dating. We get frustrated if the person driving ahead of us is traveling at the speed limit yet have the arrogance to complain when we get a ticket for going too fast. We will learn who we are only when we eliminate these distractions, taking the time to look at ourselves, our actions, and their impact.

For example, what is the impact on our children of our unwillingness to say no to them? They grow up without boundaries and consequently lack respect for people, places, and things. They pay the ultimate price because they end up disillusioned about their world. The world can be a very unkind place to people who don't understand, value, and uphold boundaries.

One of the most powerful ways to discover our truth about ourselves is by journaling. It needn't be done on a daily basis, although that can yield rich results. When we write things down, we become clear about them. By emptying our thoughts onto paper (it could also be on a computer, though I prefer to scribe them by hand), we can clearly see what is going on in our mind. I have been liberated by distinguishing fact from story; ferreting out double standards that were at play; and teasing out my personal values, belief structures, and areas where I had been afraid to own my deeper desires.

Journaling is invaluable as a resource, which is one of the reasons that I ask you to complete the powerful questions within each chapter of this book and log them anonymously on my Website. There you can read others' answers and insights, through which you will learn that you are not alone in your thinking. You will discover many different perspectives from sharing your own in a safe and anonymous forum.

You are invited to join others in this amazing journey of liberation and self-discovery. The opportunity exists for you to be of service to others through your own sharing. We are all born into a group, our family. We socialize in groups, we learn in groups, we play in groups, and we are wounded in groups. We also have to find healing in a group setting. The Website offers a safe beginning for that healing.

> To create movement in your life, answer the
> following question:
>
> **What are you unwilling to say no to and
> what impact is that having on your life?**
>
> To gain a deeper understanding, please go to
> relationshipexcellence.com to post your thoughts
> and read responses from others who are also
> committed to creating relationship excellence.

When the writing is on the wall, read it

We tend to fool ourselves in the initial stages of dating. We
let things slide that normally would bother us; we knowingly alter our threshold of acceptance. If we really like
the person we're dating and discover they are irresponsible
with money, we think they'll get better and eventually
change. Or we just chalk it up as no big deal, because we
really like them and we're insecure in the relationship.
We don't challenge them to look at their behavior and
its potential impact. We fear that doing so will hurt the
relationship. In reality, it would illuminate whether we
are in the right relationship, and if we are, would make
it stronger. We shouldn't be shocked when our spouse
blames us for ruining their life if they trash-talked their ex
at the beginning of our relationship.

Imagine, for example, that you have just started dating someone. It is clear to you that they're being reserved and withholding information. Why, when you know this, would you keep the relationship going without challenging the behavior? If they're being secretive, is it because they're afraid? Or is their secrecy based in deceit? It would serve you to challenge the behavior, instead of assuming that you know what it means.

Most people are so afraid of rejection, they let a concern like this go, telling themselves it will go away in time or they'll deal with it later. However, no one truly lets things go until they have resolution; if they simply bury the concern, it will fester and grow. When it does resurface — and it will — it will carry a new, heftier price tag.

At the beginning of a relationship, women often ask for too little. Then, once the relationship deepens, they may seem to ask for too much. Many women want a relationship so much, they look the other way when their man's behavior bothers them. Once the relationship has deepened, they naturally challenge him and attempt to hold him to account; women do this because they want to be with a man who is fulfilled and true to his greatness. The feminine wants to be with a great man and can see the potential and the greatness in the masculine before many men can see it themselves. The truth is, you can challenge a man, but you cannot hold him to account. Men can hold themselves to account only if they choose to do so.

And so it begins. Most men completely misinterpret this challenge from the feminine. They see it as an attempt to control them. Reacting to this perceived control, they avoid the real issue and shut the feminine down. They stonewall the feminine, blame them, defend their own actions, protect their own interests, justify their behavior, and many times use anger in excessive ways — all to achieve this shut-down effect. This is a strategy to maintain the status quo and avoid the risk of vulnerability, and it effectively kills communication and openness in the relationship.

Further complicating the issue is the fact that women, once hooked by this drama, react to the male's shutdown by engaging in their own justification and fulfilling the male's belief that females are controlling.

This negative dance between the sexes gives "vicious cycle" its inner, essential meaning.

A friend once told me that she was shocked on her third date with a handsome man that he drove like a maniac. She really liked him, however, so she chose not to say anything about the fear she felt. She finally mentioned it much later in the relationship, asking him to slow down while driving. He became defensive, taking her request as a criticism of his skills, rather than as an expression of her fear and desire to feel safe.

What happened here? The price tag had increased dramatically. If she had confronted the issue right away, he might have responded with more openness, especially if he, too, valued the relationship. But as time passed, she had become quietly complicit in his behavior. Silence equals acceptance for many. To speak ill of it now was, to him, absurd. When the relationship ended, some years later, she was still shocked that he continued to treat her with disrespect, disregarding the impact of his behavior. Yet the writing was on the wall, way back on their third date.

We must not allow ourselves to ignore the things we have issues with. We must stay true to ourselves and our thresholds of acceptance. In communicating our needs concerning another's behavior, we often collapse who they are with their actions. It is essential for us to separate the person and their behavior. We are not our behavior, yet we are responsible for its impact, intended or otherwise. We can continue to love the person and not like their behavior. Making this distinction permits us to not take things personally and create the safety to evolve in the relationship.

A client once told me how appalled she was at the behavior of her new boyfriend. The first time she went back to his apartment with him, she noticed he had turned his stereo speakers to the wall with loud music blaring. When she asked him why, he said it was to irritate an "asshole" neighbor. She felt her initial reaction in her body. The writing was on the wall, but she ignored it. Yet, later, when they broke up, she was shocked to see that he used irrational and childish tactics. Of course she cited his being an asshole as one of the reasons for their breakup.

This woman had deceived herself into believing her love would somehow change this man's behavior. She had created an illusion in her own mind that he would never treat her the same way. Such illusions block us from seeing what is real. What we see as reality actually depends on what we are looking for at the time.

Whether we're silent or engaging, we are always impacting the space we occupy. If we're going to be the best we can be, we need to know from others how we're impacting them.

Are we willing and courageous enough to ask how the other sees us in the world? We all have blind spots. We need others to give us feedback because we may have created an impact that was not intended. It reminds me of the adage, "The road to hell is paved with good intentions."

Here's the crux of the dilemma: We judge others by their behavior, and we judge ourselves by our intentions. And unfortunately intentions are invisible to others. Furthermore, we have conscious and unconscious intentions that need to be addressed. For us to know ourselves, and thus be able to follow through on our intentions, we need a strong support group, friends who will lovingly support us and, if we're willing to empower them, who will challenge us to be the best we can be. This can happen only when we deliberately engage them to provide us with feedback and ask them to hold us to our word.

For example, my clients who want to lose weight and don't maintain their "gains" often discover that an unconscious intention is blocking them. Through the process of feedback, some realize that they have unconsciously been terrified of the possibility of deeper intimacy or the sexual desire that arises when they're fully connected to their bodies. Working through this unconscious intention and subconscious fear with the help of a strong support structure brings resolution — and the loss of those pounds. The body never lies; the mind lies like crazy. When we accept the truth that our body has for us, we tap into its innate wisdom and ultimately evolve.

The point is, when the writing is on the wall, we need to read it and pay attention to it. When we look at the wall and the writing is unintelligible, we need to get support in order to translate it.

Aligning our words and actions

We've all had the experience of doing something with an intended outcome, only to arrive at a completely different place. A prime example of this is the number of people who join a gym as a New Year's resolution, pay their membership, start off with enthusiasm, and then fall off the wagon. They deceive themselves into thinking that paying for a membership will result in achieving their goal. It is no different from buying Calvin Klein underwear and thinking it will make us look like the model on the box.

When we publicly declare an intention, and our words and our actions are not aligned, we will slip and judge ourselves and then slide farther. These judgments put us in the worse-than box, enslaving us in our pain. Without a doubt, our words can be our prison.

When we fail to keep our word to ourselves, we wield

the same kinds of judgments against ourselves as we do against others who don't keep their word with us. We have all experienced people who say one thing and do another. We, in turn, judge them for their behavior. We say they lack integrity, are unable to commit, don't care, are disrespectful, or — worse still — cannot be trusted. We are probably right. But the irony is that if we don't keep our word to ourselves, we unconsciously end up saying the same things about ourselves. Far better for us to consciously focus on ourselves and set the tone for the behavior and outcomes we truly desire.

What does it take to be committed? What does it take to align our words and our actions?

We have all been on the giving and receiving end of judgment. The only way out of the judgment trap, and consequently out of the box, is to become curious. We have to return to becoming the passive observer of our own desires, motivation, and behavior. Only from this place can we find freedom from judgment. The judgments are all part of the stories we tell ourselves. These stories take on a life of their own and we live them out as if they were true. To oversimplify things for the sake of discussion, we could say that everything can be viewed from two perspectives, love or fear. What insights would we gain if had the courage to open up the box and discover the root of our own behavior?

I believe roughly half of what people say and all of what they do. Words do help us discover deeper truths about people, but at the end of the day, it is actions that really matter. How many times can we apologize for the same behavior before we completely lose credibility? I know of people who have, in their words, done a lot of "personal work." They take workshops, courses, get coaching and even counseling. But then they hide behind fancy words and jargon to justify the same outcomes in their behavior. When their actions have created chaos, the most common excuse I hear is, "That's not who I am committed to being." Unfortunately, the bottom line is that the results they're creating are precisely what they're committed to. The same is true of us all. So if we don't like the results, we need to look inside ourselves.

That said, when we have created an unintended impact and wish to restore integrity to the situation, we need to apologize. The meaning behind the word *sorry* is lost, however, unless we back the word up with a commitment to a subsequent change in behavior — and then actually change that behavior. Consider, for example, someone who is late for a meeting and makes an excuse for it. If they're late to subsequent meetings, they show they aren't accepting responsibility for their behavior. The lack of congruence between their words and actions is damaging their relationships. When they shrug their lateness off to an unforeseen circumstance, they lose credibility, reinforcing people's experience that their word has no value. Resolution is as simple as, "I'm sorry. Next time I will ..."

When we fail to back up our apology with a change in our behavior, we get in our own way.

Inaction

In my experience, men tend to think that if a relationship isn't easy, there's something wrong with it. Women seem to operate from a desire to make relationships easy through discussions that generate understanding. The truth is, we all long to be seen, heard, and understood, though men need a little more coaxing to take part in this process. Here is a place for curiosity. What would it take for men to feel safe to engage in conversation about the relationship? When we experience this, it brings both acceptance and connection.

However, we need to have acceptance before we can have understanding. Our resistance to what is, to the situation as it is right now, is what blocks us from learning and evolving. We get everything we need in this life, not necessarily everything we want. Imagine that whatever is going on in your life right now is perfect, whether you like it or not. Perfect for your growth and evolution as an adult.

People often ask me how I can sit and listen to other people's problems day after day and not become depressed. That's an interesting question. Many professionals in the helping industry are overwhelmed by what their clients go through. I am helped by seeing everyone as creative, resourceful, and whole. I understand that at any time we are creating experiences that are spiritually designed to bring out the best in us. Now, truth is stranger than fiction, and while I feel privileged to bear witness to clients' raw truths, many of which have never been disclosed before, I absolutely trust that what's going for them in their lives is exactly what they need in facing the choice to become their best self. It is only our resistance to what that is that works against us.

In truth, transformation occurs only when we are witnessed in our truth. I actually become energized by being present to such courageous dialogues.

When I become upset about something going on in my own life, I remind myself that an opportunity to learn something profound is just around the corner if not already right in front of me. All I need to do is get out of my own way. I am blessed to have amazing people in my life with whom I can talk transparently, a process that supports me in gaining the insight I need in order to choose peace.

Relationship is all about choice. We are brought to choice: the choice to be and to explore being — the being of others and ourselves in relationship.

Acceptance is about what is, regardless of whether we like it or desire it. It is a decision to come to terms with the situation: It is what it is. If a person is overweight and unhappy about it, acceptance is taking ownership of what is without the judgment. Only once the truth is accepted can we look at the situation and understand how we arrived there. And only from there can we choose to make a plan for change.

People are afraid that if they accept what is, they will get stuck there. But actually it's the judgment that keeps us stuck. Acceptance brings peace and gives us the ability to choose how we will move forward and take action.

Inaction rules so many of us. It is perhaps one of our most limiting traits. It is a direct result of our own thoughts. We have determined that staying put will be less painful than facing the imagined reality. Our minds have the amazing ability to take bits of information and make up an elaborate story; in fact we can make that story so powerful that we become frozen by fear. Ironically, the result, when the situation is actually played out in real life, is typically far from what we originally imagined.

We need to realize that inaction allows change to be thrust on us by outside circumstances or other people, whereas action invites the change we want. Failure to use our own power to be at choice puts us under the perceived control of another person who is using theirs. When someone uses their power and it affects us adversely, we tell ourselves that we're the victim, when in reality we inadvertently prompted the outcome by doing nothing. We are victims only when we fail to choose to initiate the change that we know we need in our own lives.

Using our power

It is irresponsible of us to claim to have "given our power away" or to blame others for "taking our power away." We always have power; we just choose whether to use it or not.

Many times we live in denial about things we know need to change. We tell ourselves things will change by themselves if left to their own devices. The problem is that change will occur — it always does — but then it will not be governed by our own actions. If we're pressured into change, out of duty, obligation, or to please others, then any change will be short-lived. The most we can do is tell our partner how their behavior impacts us and make a request for a change. This feedback is not only our right in a relationship, it is also our responsibility because we are always teaching others how we want to be treated.

I recall working with a couple who had been together for three years and were finally ready to get married. She had been a smoker throughout their relationship. He had always maintained that she would have to quit smoking if they were to get married. He didn't want to marry a smoker or have a smoker as the mother of his children. Wanting the wedding so much, this woman "quit," hiding her smoking. She was discovered several times after the wedding and her deceit eventually caused the demise of their marriage. Truth is, the relationship was set up untenably. He had accepted her as a smoker for years, expecting her to change for an event in the future. It was his agenda for change, not hers. Nothing good could come of it.

For me, feedback is the highest expression of living. Lack of feedback is like a slow death, because it cuts off our circulation: our flow of information. We all have blind spots, and we need to rely on our loved ones and others who care about us to point them out — to help us understand their impact and allow us to evolve in order to make better choices about how we want to show up in the world.

The most powerful thing we can do in a relationship is find out what the other person wants and give it to them.

I recall a situation when I was in a relationship with a woman who wiped out the bathroom sink after she used it. She liked the sink to be clean. When I stayed over, she wiped the sink out after me, sometimes asking me if I would do it. At first I didn't take her seriously. As our relationship progressed and we moved in together, she asked me to wipe out the sink every time I used it, using a special cloth she kept under the vanity for that purpose. I told her I would do it because it was important to her and that if I forgot, I wanted her to come to me and lovingly remind me instead of doing it herself and resenting me. I also asked her to thank me for remembering when she initially saw me perform the task. I have grown to enjoy a clean sink and still wipe it down after using it.

When we put up with things that don't work for us in relationship, the relationship inevitably breaks down. When we tolerate, we end up resenting the other. If we were honest with ourselves, we would admit that our resentment is about our own willingness to put up with things that don't actually work for us. We incorrectly blame the other when we're actually upset about our own inaction. Here is a choice point for taking responsibility in our own lives. It is all about choice. Tolerance breeds resentment. We then project that resentment onto the other person because it allows us to avoid looking at our responsibility for the way we have designed our relationship.

It is often touted that we are afraid of change. I believe what we're really afraid of is judgment and disapproval. To live an extraordinary life means living outside the box, and to live outside the box means being subject to the comments and ridicule that will inevitably come. Thinking and living outside the box is actually a process of expanding our box because we can now include the new experience in the box that is our experience of life and relationship. Keep in mind that the comments we receive are more a reflection of our own fears and insecurities than an accurate assessment of us. If we avoid being challenged and discount what others say, we will settle for mediocrity.

What would it mean to be in a relationship in which both of you want the best for yourselves and each other?

When nothing changes, it only gets worse

One of the most important insights we can have is that change is inevitable, growth is optional. We cannot avoid the winds of change. The best we can do is to embrace change as a natural, healthy part of life. It is going to happen anyway, so it serves us well to be fully open to it. It may be that we dislike the change. In fact, one of the ways we get in our own way is to judge change as good or as bad. It is arrogant to do so. We learn from trial and error, not from trial and success, so when we judge an experience as being bad for us, we lose the opportunity to learn from it. When we remove the judgments, we open ourselves to the learning that is there for the taking.

We always have a choice to grow from our experiences, even if we don't realize it. Our innate resistance to growth is one of our largest hindrances and is born of fear.

A friend of mine was downsized out of her job after eleven years. Throughout those years, she had talked about writing a cookbook. She knew that her fear of failure was standing in her way. She was initially shocked by the loss of her position and therefore her livelihood. But she also recognized that it had given her an opportunity to complete her book. Stepping into this change and embracing it unleashed a creative force that surprised her. The book, which had been percolating for six years, was published within a few months. Her new perspective was to envision the change as an opportunity rather than a loss. There truly is a silver lining in every cloud.

I love the analogy that life is just a series of lessons. It is as if we're in school and the door is locked, forcing us to face the lessons life has to offer. We have no choice about the lessons that are sent to us. We do have a choice whether we will embrace and grow through them today. Resisting a life lesson means it will return to us with more force at a later date; they all do. Ultimately we will learn the lesson, whether we choose to now or later.

The good news is that the most powerful vehicle for change is relationship. Why? Because of its incredibly dynamic nature and because it provides built-in support. Ever notice how many of your experiences in relationship are similar to past relationships? It is as if the relationship somehow collects and then condenses many of life's lessons, giving us access to learning and growth.

When there's pain in a relationship, will we try to change its components or ourselves? Relationship excellence means placing our focus back on the relationship and what we're contributing to it.

Six circular arguments

Couples fight about six main things:

- money
- work
- children
- sex
- in-laws
- the relationship itself.

Being caught in one or more of these circular arguments indicates a lack of alignment in the relationship. Most people think it indicates a lack of agreement, but we can never get to agreement unless we have alignment first.

Conflicts over money are never about money; the same is true of arguments about children and sex. To continue to have conflicts about these things on the surface misses the point completely. And as Albert Einstein said, "Insanity is doing the same thing over and over again, expecting a different result."

When one of these circular arguments starts up, the outcome is predictable. We know what we're going to say, again, and what the other is going to say, again. We know the drill so well, but we and our partner are sucked back into the circle. These arguments are never resolved on their own terms because they are not about those terms: They are rooted in deeper issues that cannot be resolved from that place. We need to understand and accept that we all have different perspectives. Only from a place of acceptance and then understanding can we exit circular arguments and move naturally toward agreement. I must mention, though, that the stories we create will likely come into play yet again. We need to be ready for this, ready to drop underneath the presenting argument and explore the true nature of the story that is hindering us from the proper resolution of the conflict.

Conflicts about money in a relationship are a result of what money means to us; they are not about the actual currency itself. In our culture money represents security, control, freedom, choice, and value. Individuals' perspectives on all of this vary and thus influence behavior, sometimes radically. A couple can exit the circularity of this argument only when they are willing to explore these deeper aspects of money. Rarely do two people have the same security needs. For one person, being in debt causes an inordinate amount of stress. For the other, debt is just a normal part of life with no ill effects. Being mortgage free may provide one person with a much-needed level of security but never even register on their partner's radar screen.

The conflict arises when neither is willing to hear what it is about the other's perspective that matters to them. Acceptance in this situation will come about when the couple delves into a conversation with a high degree of curiosity about the conditions that create security for each of them. An opening can be created for mutual understanding as each of us recognizes and understands that we all have unique security needs and accepts our individual needs for what they are. Only then can we progress toward creating alignment and subsequently agreement.

Note that when the reaction of one or the other in a relationship is out of proportion to the current event, this is a signal that some past issue needs to be brought into the open and healed. This is a time for the members of a couple to be open and gentle with themselves and the other. This isn't a time for accusations. It is a time for curiosity, fascination, and discovery, which will lead to a better understanding of what the relationship needs in order to flourish.

That said, conflict is a natural process in relationship and a helpful one because it signifies the need for growth. We use words in conflict, knowing that they're powerful but perhaps not knowing that they have a particular meaning to us and a different meaning to someone else. The word *conflict* itself needs to be explored because we each bring to the relationship perspectives on conflict from our family of origin. For one it may represent isolation, loneliness, or even despair. For another it may reflect a way of conversing. Regardless, we need to be conscious of the personal distinctions and move forward from there. For some, conflict has a high emotional charge; for others it has none.

Conflict has the potential to bring closeness, connection, and healing. When we don't understand this, we create more disconnection and separation. Disconnection causes pain in the relationship, and the longer the pain is left unattended, the greater the pain and the disconnection. When conflict isn't attended to, things get worse. Avoiding the conflict is not a solution to the problem, because it simply allows it to fester and grow. Countless people think a problem will go away over time if it is just pushed aside. Not so. If we are carrying twenty extra pounds, we will not lose weight by ignoring the fact. Solving the problem requires commitment, focus, learning, care, and attention. Until then, the dissatisfaction is likely to grow and make things worse.

When we're "curious about" the conflict and move away from "judgments about" the conflict, we're on the way to aligning words and actions. The challenge is to become curious about the judgments we have and where they came from.

The difference between an observation and a judgment is that a judgment has an emotional charge attached to it.

Understanding the difference will allow us to uncover and embrace deeper truths about ourselves.

Alignment

When we argue, we are pushing for agreement: We want the other to see things our way. Arguing only illuminates the fact that we have no alignment. When we push for an agreement through argument, in any area of our lives, we're likely to encounter resistance and pushback. After all, the other person is going to champion their own view. To agree with another means to have the same opinion, and to be aligned in that opinion. That's quite different from a duality of views clashing on the way to victory.

There are two problems with opinions: First, they aren't based on positive proof, and second, they are not about direct experience. When we become attached to our opinion, we become rigid about the outcome we want. The challenge is to keep the conversation focused on resolving the issue instead of letting it be dragged into a destructive dance of who's right and who's wrong. To create alignment, we need to have congruence of intention. In fact, most people pushing for agreement really want alignment but don't know how to create it. This is yet another example of how we get in our own way.

We rarely see this key point, that we can have alignment with each other without necessarily agreeing with each other. For example, we can be aligned in the desire to be debt free but disagree on how to get there. Coming into alignment opens up options to attain the goal. A couple may not agree with all the ways of attaining the outcome because some of them may bring one or the other to an edge, which would be a signal for their own learning. However, in the process of alignment the partners can move to an outcome that serves the relationship. The focus shifts to something bigger than each person in the relationship: to creating a relationship that feels great for both.

As we move forward, it is important to recognize that the six circular arguments are not really arguments. They are simply indications of deeper personal needs or wants. They are excellent opportunities to create alignment.

Arguments about the children are opportunities to create alignment in what to teach them, in how to model ways of being in the world that will help them flourish.

Arguments about in-laws are opportunities to restate and reinforce healthy boundaries. A husband who refuses to intervene when his mother interferes in his family is choosing not to align with his wife. This discord can be resolved only when he moves from argument to alignment with her about what their family relationship needs. This is a man who has not severed his ties with his mother and therefore is not fully available to his wife. The conflict has nothing to do with the mother and it is unfair to make it so. In fact this lack of alignment between the couple will damage extended family relationships as well.

Arguments about sex are opportunities to deal with issues of control, anger, shame, and at times resistance to vulnerability. When one person in the relationship feels powerless in any way, be it about money, time, or whether they are taken seriously, one of the most powerful places for them to exercise control is in the bedroom. To argue about sex is futile. Failing to deal with the lack of sexual intimacy will ultimately fragment the relationship. Relationships need a great sex life.

Arguments about work are excellent opportunities to align priorities and define where we get validation and acknowledgement.

Arguments about the relationship itself are opportunities to address a lack of connection and failure to maintain and renew the relationship vision.

In conclusion, words without actions have no currency. Alignment in relationship is the vehicle for changes, moving us toward our relationship vision.

To create movement in your life, answer the following question:

What is the writing on the wall that you are refusing to read in your relationship?

To gain a deeper understanding, please go to relationshipexcellence.com to post your thoughts and read responses from others who are also committed to creating relationship excellence.

5

Three Relationship Killers

Anger isn't negative; how it's expressed can be

THREE THINGS WILL ULTIMATELY KILL a relationship if left unresolved: anger, withholding, and insecurity. These represent the proverbial nails in the coffin of a relationship that is on its way out. Ironically, it is how we deal with them that makes them so detrimental. We have the ability to take charge of our feelings, and to control our bodily states, yet we don't take responsibility for doing so. Instead we blame, protect, defend, and justify our behavior. Unfortunately, this simply serves to entrench us deeper in our disarray, creating a more thorough stuckness.

Anger

If I feel angry, the feeling is mine, because it is in my body. As with any feeling, the anger is attempting to inform me about something. Nobody else can make me feel angry; the feeling is truly coming from within. Yes, there is cause and effect: Someone does something and I react. But I nevertheless remain responsible for the response in my body — and for how I choose to respond. We will focus on anger later in this chapter.

Withholding

Withholding information is also a choice. It is our own decision, and ours alone. Many times it is not what we say but what we don't say that kills a relationship. We need to do two things to counteract the detrimental effect of withholding information. The first is to take responsibility for how we fail to do this and to understand the impact of not doing so. The second is to look at creating the conditions for truth telling in a relationship.

If we have an affair, the concealment of the affair takes energy. That energy is taken away from the relationship. The more energy taken away, the weaker the relationship becomes. Ironically, when we withhold, we withdraw and then project on the other that they aren't available or cannot handle what's going on. Yet all the while it is our behavior that is creating the effect. Anything that we withhold serves to disrupt and weaken the relationship.

There are other aspects that we can withhold. One of my biggest personal breakthroughs came one day after hanging up on my father. I was walking down the hall at my office complaining yet again that my father was a drunk. A colleague, Anne-Shirley, was passing me just at that time. A large, powerful woman with a huge heart, she grabbed me by my shirt, backed me into the wall, and said, "All you have ever wanted from that man is for him to accept you as you are and that's the one thing you won't give him."

Well, that was a wake-up call, and I woke up. It showed me that the only thing missing in my relationship with my father was what I was withholding. That intervention was one of the most loving things anyone has ever given me. The relationship was transformed in that moment. I was the one who fundamentally changed. And the shift it caused in my attitude to my father and my new responses to him caused him to respond differently and subsequently change.

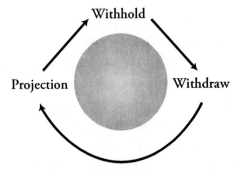

Whenever we make the decision to withhold information, we essentially decide to kill off the relationship bit by bit. To conceal the information requires us to withdraw from the relationship because our energy is focused on the withhold.

Next we project onto the person some fabricated story to justify our decision to withhold. Then we withhold that projection from the person and around we go again, all the time withdrawing farther and farther away from the relationship.

Insecurity

If I am feeling insecure, it is my feeling, my mental state. Insecurity is rooted in fear. We all want to feel peaceful. When we're afraid, we will either attempt to quell it by controlling the outside conditions and people or by controlling our inner state so we can return to peace. We may make our insecurities about the other, but in truth, if the fear is going on in our body, then we're responsible for seeing what the body/mind is offering to tell us.

When we're in a situation with the potential for anger and conflict and we're afraid of conflict, we may go into an animated state, trying to make everybody happy as a distraction. Or we may withdraw and go numb, exhibiting no apparent feelings about the situation. Insecurities are formed against a backdrop of the comparisons and evaluations we make. We can instantly take ourselves out of the game by making up stories about how we don't measure up. Jealousy is a good example. When we feel jealous, we focus on our supposedly disloyal partner or the person we think is threatening the relationship. We are actually projecting our personal insecurity on another.

Anger revisited

Anger can be the cause or manifestation of problems related to the relationship killers of withholding and insecurity. Let's look at this relationship killer in more detail.

Anger is by far the most misunderstood of all of our emotions. The inherent negativity in the way many people express it gives it a bad press. And we have all had painful experiences with this emotion, whether on its receiving or giving end, experiences that have reinforced its raw nature in us. One way or another, we have all been blamed, wronged, ridiculed, or shut down by the anger of another. And one way or another, we have allowed our anger to do the same to others.

Anger is such a powerful attribute that some professional athletes are hired simply for their capacity to demonstrate it in a game. The sole purpose of some hockey players is to antagonize opposing players in order to "turn the game around."

We're also inundated with attitudes about anger through the media, but in a dramatically convoluted form. For example, a double standard is unfortunately perpetuated with respect to men and women. The media portray women who express anger as falling victim to their emotions. Men are portrayed as fools for the way they express anger.

Anger is the one emotion we project outwardly and place on others. We blame others for the way we feel and make them responsible for our state.

Anger is one of the most natural of emotions. Just watch how babies or little children naturally express it. We arrive in this world hardwired with the full range of emotions. The problem arises when we try to override this hardwiring with judgments about emotions.

For example, in North American culture, men are allowed to be angry but must not cry. Women are allowed to cry but must not be angry. How ridiculous is that? Why do we force ourselves to live outside the parameters of our own natural emotions? Anger is not gender based or gender biased.

We all need and have full access to the complete range of emotional expression. For example, anger is one of the five stages involved in grieving any loss. It is a necessary and natural part of grief. Accepting anger as a natural response to loss is crucial for our healing and well being.

Sometimes anger is the only way adolescents can break an unhealthy bond with parents or other siblings. It is a brilliant strategy for creating the distance they need for their growth, separation, and individuation from the family system. However, many adolescents never transcend this anger stage. As they emerge into adulthood, they usually fall into one of two categories. Some become socially polite and yet remain distant, experiencing difficulties in adult relationships because they're unable to work through their unresolved issues. Others remain entrenched in their anger, making themselves unapproachable. The latter strategy is one I often see manifested as spite. The relationship has an aura of malevolence to it: "You hurt me, so now I'll hurt myself; you'll see" is their message to the world.

Unresolved anger at parents is one of the main reasons adults screw up their own lives. They are unconsciously robbing their parents of the opportunity to boast about their children doing well in the world. This is one of the most profound ways adults get in their own way. Hanging on to this unresolved anger infects all of their current and future relationships.

Some couples take pride in never fighting. These are the couples who should be the most worried. A relationship lacks depth and true communication when anger is not expressed directly. Yes, anger can be a very good thing. It is good because it is a signal calling us forth into action, telling us something is wrong and that we need to pay attention to it, now. Anger, when expressed responsibly, has the power to unite and join couples in amazing ways. Amazing because when two people each take responsibility for their own anger, they find ways to express its energy in healthy, uplifting ways. Underneath their anger they will find clarity about the issue and the request they need to make, opening a powerful avenue for communication.

The dictionary definition of the word *anger* doesn't describe it as *a negative emotion.* However, I suspect if we were to poll our friends and colleagues, at least ninety percent of them, both men and women, would say anger is negative in the context of relationship.

In the definition of anger as *an emotional response to a perceived injustice,* the crucial word and idea is *perceived.* Many times the anger is just a result of a situation or a story we've made up in our minds. How many times have people said to us, "Why are you angry about that?"

or "That's not worth getting angry over"? These comments, though probably not helpful at the time, illustrate
that those around us see the situation differently. We're
all victims of our perception, and perception is fickle and
relative to the individual. We need to be conscious of
this. Again, *anger is an emotional response to a* perceived
injustice.

Powerful though it is, anger is no more powerful than
love, and in fact anger is inherently related to love. If we
don't care about someone, we're not likely to be angered
by them. The negative perception of anger needs to be
transformed if we are to truly deepen our relationships. It
is the way we express anger in our culture that has negative consequences. Anger in and of itself is a wonderful
emotion.

Most of us grew up in an environment where anger
was either expressed directly or indirectly along with fear,
shame, and trepidation. These expressions are deeply
ingrained in us, as a result. In my home, my father had a
monopoly on the expression of anger. He would scream,
yell, and at times use physical violence; at that time
we all generally felt terrified. Our own anger was covered
up with fear — the fear of being punished. As a result,
our anger went underground, where it would inflict great
damage.

When my father wasn't around, my mother had her
own forms of expressing anger. She would resort to bang-
ing cupboards and slamming doors. She was also a master

of communicating her anger with a look, something I call "cold anger." It is silent, effective, and difficult to explain to others, but it is an expression of anger nonetheless.

Our parents' anger becomes intrinsic to us and takes shape in us later on in life. For example, I may perceive that someone is looking at me in cold anger, triggering that old uncomfortable experience from my childhood and thus triggering instant anger and discomfort within me.

When our anger is triggered in this way, it is our signal to go deep and look within ourselves, to take ownership of the reaction and discover what it is trying to teach us. Silence is not necessarily an indication that all is well; it could be a signal of impending emotional turmoil.

When my mother was frustrated with my father, she would sometimes threaten to leave him. This both thrilled and terrified me. I fantasized that she would leave and take me with her. The petrifying reality, however, was that I had no idea whether she really would leave — or whether she would take me with her or leave me behind. Later, when I was dating in early adulthood, I grew immediately angry if someone threatened to leave me. It immediately triggered anger. I never fully understood the depth of this reaction until I unearthed the emotional connection to the earlier fear that my mother would leave me. Only once I was able to take responsibility for this reaction, to understand why it was happening, and to heal the wound, was I able to eliminate being triggered in this way.

Our unwillingness to do this kind of deep personal work is one of the ways we get in our own way.

You see, my *perceived injustice* was that someone would leave and abandon me, and the anger was my reaction to that. Once my wound was healed in this area, this kind of threat no longer had an emotional charge attached to it. I could respond from a grounded place.

When we feel the emotion of anger in our body, it is informing us, in that moment, that we are experiencing an injustice. We feel angry when:

- we don't get our way
- we feel hopeless or helpless in a situation
- we want another person or group to do things our way (because we think we're right)
- we're told we're wrong
- we aren't allowed to be angry
- we feel controlled
- someone tells us a truth we don't like
- we feel disrespected or unappreciated
- our opinions aren't heard
- our feelings are denied
- someone crosses a boundary that we've set.

The provocation or the experience of the emotion itself is irrelevant. What matters is how and what we do with the feeling. As creatures of habit, we will resort to our predefined, scripted patterns unless we're ready to learn about them and create new and more effective ways of being.

We are not our behavior. We have ultimate freedom and choice over how we want to behave; we must not let behavior define us. Breaking out of our conditioning can be frightening. It takes courage to step into the realm of uncertainty and not knowing — to own our anger and take responsibility for the impact of how we express it.

The beauty of anger is that in moments of perceived powerlessness it makes us feel all-powerful. The energy is strong and palpable in our body. It causes us to think we are right, often with righteous indignation.

There were times in my childhood when my parents would argue and one of us children would say something that tipped the scales of frustration in one parent or the other. When my mother would lose it, my father would say, "Now look at how you've upset your mother!" We would always feel terrible about it. Thus was the link established that we were somehow responsible for another person's feelings. Sound familiar?

Most men have great difficulty being with a woman's anger. Men need to learn to stand in a woman's anger and love her through her anger. They are unable to do this because when their mother was angry in front of them when they were boys, they were flooded with the intensity of her emotion and ended up feeling afraid. A boy relies on his mother to feel safe and secure. When she becomes angry, his whole world stands to fall apart. Furthermore, if the boy's father is absent during this time, or if he is unable to stand in his wife's anger, the boy will scurry about trying to fix the situation. If he can't make it better (which he can't because he is a boy), then he is at risk of debilitating fear. Confronted by a woman who is angry, men are triggered into the memory of these past events.

Boys are taught that they aren't supposed to feel angry. So they deny that any anger exists until it runs their life. A man will act his fear out in front of a woman who is expressing her anger by attempting to overpower her anger with more of their own, or by withdrawing completely from the experience. Both of these reactions only serve to escalate a woman's anger, which may go underground, to be released with greater power later. When anger is engaged in overpowering other emotions, particularly the ones that create intimacy and closeness, a relationship is really in danger.

I recall working with a man who, in his words, had "transcended" his anger. At one point, his wife was angry with him because he had traded in her car (which she loved) without her knowledge. He chose to see her as irrational and even mentally ill, rather than as a partner who was simply angry about the situation. He was totally disconnected from the impact of his behavior. He was blind to the real transcendence that she was offering him: the transcendence of self-knowledge. His denial eventually led to their separation, with enormous consequences to his wife and children.

Anger is experienced physically in the body as a flash of heat; and hence it is deemed to be a hot emotion. Just think of all the phrases associated with it: hot under the collar, all fired up, burning up inside, hot-tempered. When we express anger outwardly, it contains all of this intensity and heat. Like a log placed next to burning coals, our words may be inflammatory, sparking heat in another. Our face goes red, we sweat, and our heart pounds. We can learn how to be present for another during their anger when we take ownership of our reaction, both emotionally and physically and become curious about what's going on for us. This idea is crucial.

We tend to fall into a hole, over and over, when we take anger personally and defend, justify, and blame in order to protect ourselves from the perceived attack. We can stop taking things personally only when we know who we are and what we stand for. We can get out of the hole through deep personal exploration, an understanding of our own faulty conditioning, and the knowledge that while we're responsible for the impact of our behavior, we're never responsible for what is going on in another person's body.

There is something beautiful about anger: It calls us forth to learn about ourselves — about our own boundaries and how to set them. However, if we have been shamed in any way for being angry, and most of us have, or even were witness to someone else being shamed, we are in danger of denying and burying our anger, losing sight of this gift. How many times have we heard it said, or said it ourselves, when referring to a possible confrontation, "It's not worth it. Why bother? It won't make any difference anyway."

If we tend to bury anger, we do so deep within us. But our bodies aren't designed to keep anger in. I have seen countless situations where the attempt to do so has manifested itself in physical disease. I have also been witness to amazing healing when people have fully expressed their anger. I recall a man who lost his hearing in childhood and could hear only with hearing aids. After an intense process of releasing emotions about things he had experienced in childhood, his hearing came back. I witnessed his joy as he heard his children for the very first time without his hearing aids.

Anger will leak out as sarcasm, bitterness, an unwillingness to let go, and resentment. Sarcasm is often referred to as a cutting sense of humor. The dictionary definition of the word is *the tearing of flesh*. It is no wonder we find it so painful to be on the receiving end of sarcasm. Chronic lateness is a classic manifestation of passive anger. We are all in control of how we manage our time. It is a major kiss off when we're chronically late for appointments and hide behind excuses.

Imploding and exploding

When dealing with anger, people tend to internalize it (implode) or externalize it (explode). Some will actually do both, employing the bottle up and blow approach. Dealing with anger in any of these ways hinders a congruent flow of emotions; it results in a volatility that is not conducive to connection and communication. The smallest thing may set someone off; perhaps it is completely irrelevant, and boom, the rage that comes out is completely out of proportion to the situation. We spray our anger at the people in front of us, inundating them with our intensity and emotions. And interestingly, some of us do so only to the people we love the most.

Further, we can be with another's anger only to the degree to which we can be with our own. This is why so many therapists attempt to shut down a client's anger.

Anger is versatile, expressing itself in many styles:

○ Bottle and Blow, already mentioned, where we hold it in till one little things tips the scales of injustice.

○ The Intimidator, whose arrogance and fear dominate the landscape, daring people to engage in their wrath.

○ The Interrogator, whose rapid-fire questions give people no chance to respond.

○ Mr. Nice Guy, whom we know you cannot trust because he's just too sugary sweet.

○ Angry All the Time, the person who is so stuck in the emotion that their fuse is always on a slow burn, and we think, "Better stay clear of this one."

A fundamental understanding of our own anger — of its source and how it is expressed — is imperative in our ability to surpass its limiting and imprisoning nature.

I believe today's popular anger-management approach has it all wrong. The challenge is not to manage our anger but to understand its call to action, stepping in and taking responsibility for it and ultimately dictating the outcome we want. We're always responsible for our impact, intended or not, and consequently most of us have much to clean up in the way we have expressed our anger in the past. If we are blind to the origin and cause of our anger, we will be blind to real choice. Whether we realize it or not, we are always at choice.

To create movement in your life, answer the following question:

How do you express anger and what is it costing your relationship?

To gain a deeper understanding, please go to relationshipexcellence.com to post your thoughts and read responses from others who are also committed to creating relationship excellence.

We need to create a space in relationship where anger can be expressed. The bottom line is that we don't have the right to express our anger at another person without their consent. This may sound absurd, but the truth is, it's unfair and immoral for us to injure others emotionally with our anger. We violate the other when we direct our anger at them without their agreement. It is that simple.

Now let me be clear, and perhaps this is where the line is blurred and consequently crossed so many times: There is a distinct difference between expressing our anger in front of someone, where they are simply bearing witness to it, and directing our anger at them.

Anger versus rage

As discussed, expressing anger is crucial. Doing so in a misguided way, however, can be destructive. This distinction needs to be recognized. However, before deepening this learning, let's take a look at the difference between anger and rage.

Rage may be defined as a repressed anger violently expressed against self and/or others. We have already discussed our ability to repress anger, and the consequences of doing so. Road rage is a prime example of this. It is a manifestation of anger presenting itself as a big boom, a violently outward expression. It is typically the result of a non-issue, a small inconsequential event that ignites the fuel of rage standing at the ready. This is what we commonly refer to as anger; but it is not anger. It is rage in its purest of forms. Our confusion over the two causes great difficulty in our culture.

Anger is in the moment. It is instantaneous, showing up in our bodies immediately. Rage, on the other hand, is all-encompassing and overwhelming. We become blind with rage and it colors our judgment.

One evening as I was leaving my office, I noticed that the aerator in the fish tank in the lobby was not working well. I thought of trying to fix it but decided to tackle it in the morning. When I returned the next day, the biggest fish in the tank was floating upside down. In the moment, I felt angry. One part of me knew I needed to have inspected the aerator the night before, and another part was angry that the company contracted to monitor the aquarium had not kept to its schedule. The anger was mine. The emotional response informed me that I needed to trust and follow my own instincts. I had thought of contacting the fish guy a week earlier and hadn't. I had thought of checking the aerator and didn't. The person I was angry with, ultimately, was me. I took the opportunity, revealed to me by my anger, to do things differently from then on.

The experience served me well. Rage in this instance would be calling up the guy responsible and yelling at him and making him wrong for the incident and demanding that he "do something." When we're enraged we are often stuck in our own need to be right, which evokes the need to punish. If punishment was part of our upbringing, as it was for most of us, we will often unconsciously punish others when we feel wronged. Even though at a fundamental level we know punishment does not work, we will employ it as a strategy for evening up the score.

By the time anger shows up in many relationships, its expression is often a last-ditch effort to communicate. Many times the initial lack of effective communication to resolve an issue that results in the anger is rooted in our being too polite and too nice, out of a fear of conflict. Unfortunately, at this point the anger has been festering for so long, there is additional anger over that fact, and the outcome of all this is usually messy. Our moment-to-moment anger is repressed out of politeness, but the result, when our system is full and we erupt without notice, is anything but polite.

Misunderstanding anger

I believe we need to pick our battles in relationship. My whole point is that the anger we feel, or won't let ourselves feel, is designed to inform us of something. The anger is still not about the other. It is our vehicle for self-discovery. It is our opportunity to learn about our boundaries and to speak up about our needs.

When we misunderstand our anger and judge it, we deny it and write it off. We're not angry, we might say; we're just frustrated or upset. This is a clever camouflage for our own discomfort with the feeling in our body and with our responsibility to take ownership of it. This is one of the major ways we deny our anger. We downgrade it and minimize it with one or more of the following words: frustrated, bothered, miffed, irritated, disappointed, pissed off, upset, mad, and enraged. All of which point to the fact that the anger is not being owned.

By contrast, some people are so stuck in their anger that there appears to be no separation between them and the emotion. "She's an angry woman," we might say. While this is not accurate, because there's no such thing as an angry person, there are people who unfortunately become stuck in the emotion and appear that way.

When we implode, we hold our anger inside and turn the energy against ourselves. We do this as a result of self-doubt and of questioning our own judgments. Our level of self-criticism is high in this situation; we are lethargic and feel burdened.

Addictions are the ultimate manifestations of inward-directed anger. Smoking is known for its devastating health effects, yet despite being educated about these risks, many choose to continue to smoke. I chuckle at the irony when I pass hospital buildings with hordes of staff and patients standing outside puffing away. When I soften my gaze, though, I see the bigger picture. All those people fuming at the mouth like smoke stacks have something smolder-ing inside them. Their smoking is a way of venting. I wonder how many of them feel trapped in their life, in their jobs, in their relationships, and their debts, both emotional and financial. Do they simply feel angry with themselves? As a way of pointing the anger inward, they spew smoke outward.

When I think of all the "addicts" I have worked with, including myself, I see that the underlying message we arrived at is that we were all living some form of self-hatred. At times it has been our own inherent gifts and talents that we have loathed the most. Why is it that so many of the celebrities we idolize for their artistic or athletic contributions seem hell-bent on self-destruction? Possibly we are the same as they, only we get to be less public about it.

By far the worst and perhaps most detrimental form of anger being "acted in" is depression. I see depression as anger without the enthusiasm. When we become depressed, we're actually repressing the feeling of anger and likely other feelings as well; we keep it all in, under the lid. It is no wonder we feel heavy, tired, and lethargic when depression sets in. It actually takes more energy to hold this anger, this energy, in, than if we simply let it out. We expend energy to contain anger because we judge the anger to be bad and wrong. Only action and responsible expression will release and cure depression.

Inward and outward expressions of anger are different ways of achieving the same outcome, that of moving away from the tension we feel in our body. We're so uncomfortable with tension that we'll do almost anything to distract ourselves from it. Yet staying in the tension, taking responsibility for it, and opening ourselves up to what it has to teach us are critical if we're going to grow and change as humans.

The idea of being an addict is important. We shouldn't automatically take ourselves out of the picture. To some degree we're all addicts. Perhaps not like the ones we see in the street, or our alcoholic uncle Reggie, but more subtle ones who choose to take our poison in other ways. Think about this. If we cannot miss our reality show on TV, then what is running our life? If we cannot get to the office without our morning latte, what is running our life? If we cannot get ourselves out of a circular argument, stop the cycle of debt we're drowning in, go a day without checking our e-mails, or leave our BlackBerry at home on vacation, what is running our life? We tend to view things in extremes, and many times the subtle things can be much more detrimental to us because they are hidden from our conscious awareness.

All of these addictions, regardless of their intensity, take us out of the moment. They are our distractions. Ironically, all of the ways we try to escape our feelings, to avoid the tension and feeling bad, inevitably bring us right back to what we're trying to escape. We are pleasure-seeking, pain-avoiding creatures, yet through these efforts we in fact ultimately create more pain and less pleasure. We shop because it makes us feel better; it is our distraction, perhaps our addiction. Then we're left with financial debts, and soon thereafter, when the novelty of the new purchase has diminished, our original hardship and pain resurface.

True self-esteem

To the surprise of many, self-esteem is directly linked to anger. When we hold that anger in, deny our feelings, and live with judgments, we cultivate an emotional state that does not allow for self-esteem. Further, we and others know we're being inauthentic. This in turn keeps us from feeling good about ourselves and from being able to achieve esteem. Well, let's break it down very simply. We esteem what we value. To have self-esteem means to value ourselves, our being. If we don't value ourselves, including our emotions, we will never have self-esteem, period.

How can we feel good about ourselves when we know we're not being true to ourselves? When we know we're living with anger, resentment, guilt, or shame and doing nothing about it, we're not able to hold our self in high value. To mask the pain we will often engage in an activity to take us out of the tension.

Harnessing the power of anger

Without question, anger is a powerful emotion, one that seems to come forth almost on its own. It appears seemingly unbid when we need to set a boundary or when we have been denied something we want. The good news is that we can harness the inherent strength of anger to facilitate powerful change. We can use its power as energy to make things happen — for example, to prove to ourselves and others that a job can be accomplished.

We need to know what our anger feels like in our bodies and what it is connected to. We need to find healthy ways of expressing it, so we can get to what's really beneath it. There is always a request buried below our anger. When we vent our anger at another person, they will likely react to the energy of the anger and consequently miss the message. We have effectively shot the recipient and the messenger — ourselves. Many people subscribe to the old saying, don't go to bed angry. If we aren't able to express our anger in healthy ways within the relationship, we will go to bed because we're angry.

I have worked with many couples facing the issue of infidelity. Obviously this betrayal of relationship brings a tremendous amount of anger into the relationship. In fact, I see having an affair as a form of passive anger being acted out. I'd go one step further and say that unexpressed anger in relationship is the main cause of sexual and intimacy difficulties. Yes, I'll go so far as to say it is the withholding of the expression of anger that stops us from being intimate. When we suffer all the little injustices and are unable to resolve and complete communication transactions, we pull away and effectively communicate a f*#k you — or rather, more to the point, I won't f*#k you. Both parties are responsible and have played a part when an affair has occurred.

My prescription where men have been unfaithful and when both parties are willing to work through the feelings is to engage them in the practice of Tantrum Yoga. Couples who have taken this approach experience intense healing and connection. The man stands in front of his partner with a pillow on his chest (preferably a very thick sofa pillow). The woman beats on this pillow with her fists while screaming out all of her hurt: her sense of betrayal, her anger, sadness, and whatever else she has stored inside. And he is to stand there, without taking any of it personally, letting her vent. He is to see it as her pain and acknowledge it as such. The rules are that she cannot scratch or kick him, or knee him in the groin.

Typically, within twenty minutes she will sense a release and will fall into his arms sobbing, feeling as though a huge weight has been lifted. Some may need to repeat this, and some even several times. Regardless, this exercise allows for a truly positive, effective, and controlled release of the built-up anger. It not only reopens the avenue of communication, it also helps repair the fractured relationship.

If it was the woman who cheated, the man needs to take the bulk of his anger and rage to other men first, before clearing his hurt with the woman. Failure to do so will inevitably leave him stuck in his anger at himself, the other man, or the woman. We can truly let something go only when we have the felt sense of feeling heard and validated!

To create movement in your life, answer the following question:

What unfinished business do you need to clean up? What's keeping you from doing so?

To gain a deeper understanding, please go to relationshipexcellence.com to post your thoughts and read responses from others who are also committed to creating relationship excellence.

Saying no — and yes

The beauty of anger is that it signifies a boundary has been crossed or a boundary needs to be established. We become frustrated and bent out of shape over boundaries. We think people "should" know better, or we may have even told them once, so what's their problem — why are they "purposefully" doing this? The problem is that our boundaries and the other's boundaries are just that, mine and theirs, and it is up to us to enforce them.

Think of boundaries as self-imposed limits. People will push, and continue to do so, until our internal limit has been reached. The flash of anger we feel tells us either that our limit has been crossed or that one needs to be set, firmly. The challenge, though, is that we assume others know our limits and we blame and make them wrong for crossing them. The reality is, only we know our limits and boundaries and it is our responsibility to make others aware of them.

We must be careful, however, not to do so in that moment of anger. When we set limits from that place, people will inevitably react to the energy and miss the point. When we set a new boundary for the first time, people may react and give us flack, particularly if they're used to seeing us in a certain way or having things their way. In reality, when we set new boundaries, it comes across as if we are changing the rules. Consequently, until we are fully clear about our own limits and boundaries, people will test and pressure us to return to the way we have always been.

This behavior is actually quite good, in two ways: First, it tells us we have had an impact, and second, it allows us to see what we're fully committed to.

Saying no is a distinct boundary in itself, one that many people allow others to cross. That is, we want to say no, but don't. Or we say no and people don't take us seriously. In these cases we need to look at the energy and commitment behind the no. We have great difficulty in saying no because we have all felt the pain of being told no in our life. Don't underestimate this. A situation in which something that we wanted was denied to us may have changed the course of our life.

It is also important to remember that it takes two to say yes in a relationship and only one to say no. We want to spare the people we care about the pain of disappointment and often end up suffering instead. Just remember that saying no to another is saying yes to ourselves. People's reactions to our boundaries are about them; we don't have to adjust our boundaries because others are unhappy with them. Our work is to be clear about ourselves and our needs, as we teach others how to treat us.

This does require tact, however, and an understanding of the other's emotional response. Many do not respond well to your telling them that they cannot do something, regardless of the fact that it is your boundary. This immediately brings resistance and objection. The most effective way to set a boundary is for us to say, "If you want to behave that way, go ahead — just not with me." This way we aren't telling the other what they can or cannot do; we're simply setting the boundary for our own tolerance. So anger, withholding, and insecurity are often collapsed into one silent (or not so silent) killer. Pulling them apart and understanding these elements will create great freedom of choice for you.

To create movement in your life, answer the following question:

What insecurity is keeping you from entering fully into your relationship?

To gain a deeper understanding, please go to relationshipexcellence.com to post your thoughts and read responses from others who are also committed to creating relationship excellence.

6

The Work of Men

A man should never change his mind
just to please a woman

IT IS RARE FOR A man to take the lead in a relationship today. That has long been the woman's domain, but women have grown increasingly weary of carrying the burden for the health of the relationship.

It is time for men to grow up. Men miss the point — and the full experience of relationship — because they lack the fortitude to step in and join with their partners to co-create what they want. Men make it so easy for women to blame and point fingers at them and then resent them for doing so. The complaint I hear repeatedly from men is that women are trying to change them. I don't believe this to be true at all and I can understand how men end up thinking that way. The truth is, women want men to participate more in the relationship. Ironically, the more men participate in co-creating the relationship, the more they will change.

The caveman era has long been over and so has the notion of the passive male figure. Men must awaken to the idea that they are responsible for creating the relationship they have, or the one they don't have. They must get over the notion that emotions exist to be suppressed. They must allow those emotions to surface and embrace them for the gift they are.

The place of fear

Of all of the emotions that men aren't supposed to feel, fear is the biggest. Ironically, though, men live and make decisions from a place of fear while masquerading as being full of confidence. Men never make a good decision when it is based on fear. Fear blurs the objectivity they need to gauge the situation correctly; it fogs their judgment with emotions. The only way for men to break through their fear is to face the fact that fear isn't even real. It is the dressing up of societal and perhaps gender stereotypes as fear.

Most men do not have a strong social network. Yet they cannot face their fears alone and need to remember that by not paying attention to and resolving how fear is running their life, they get in their own way. Many are squeamish about support groups, but they are exactly the tool they need.

Most men live alone in their world. Most men are more invested in their ego and its need to be right than they are in being open and challenged. A man cannot learn and grow from this place of ego; he will remain infantile and boyish if he tries to do so, stagnating in his reactions to the world and to others in the world.

It is time for men to become conscious of the new reality that relationships aren't working for them either. Women need to feel a man's love. When a man withholds his love, a woman withers and withdraws and the relationship dies. Women are susceptible to being drawn into fantasy romance novels and movies to fill the void. Imagine being the kind of man your wife would fantasize about having an affair with? Imagine being the kind of man you would feel great about being? The kind of man who is a role model in his commitment to principles and values — the kind who is the hero your spouse and children need you to be.

Becoming a man

The problem is that boys no longer go through rites of passage. So many of them are abandoned in the transition from boyhood to manhood. Few boys are schooled in the art of becoming a man and thus lack the discipline required to traverse that crucial passage. As a boy reaches puberty, he naturally pulls away from his mother. It is part of his thirst for independence. If he lacks the presence of a strong and focused male figure to guide him in the way of being a man, he will be drawn into a push-and-pull struggle with his mother. This then becomes the basis of all his future interactions with women, something I con-

tinually witness in my work. A boy needs to be walked
through his fears of the responsibility that is a part of
manhood. He needs other men to guide him in this
process; otherwise he will develop through a veil of self-
doubt and a lack of assurance.

When a man has been disconnected from his father,
when he hasn't been taught by him to become a great
man, he lacks the knowledge that he is truly loved. A man
needs to feel loved by another man before he can fully
accept the love of a woman. He will search for love from
a woman over and over again and yet never surrender
into it when he gets it. Most men therefore have much
work ahead of them, because much of their emotional
hardship is rooted in lack of father love and acceptance.

Many boys and young men are brought up with emotionally or physically absent fathers. As a result, they do
not know the deepest part of who they are. Facing fears
is a painful process at any age. When they don't face
these imagined demons as adolescents, they have to portray themselves to the world through a false mask as
men. This mask is one of arrogance or soft timidity.

I hated my father while growing up. I hated the way he
treated me. I hated the way he was in the world. I hated
that I couldn't connect with him. The worst thing anyone
could ever say to me was, "You're just like your father."

I spent my adolescence and young adulthood trying
my best not to be him. Ironically, that which we fear, we
become. My worst fears had come true by the time I was
twenty-eight. All I could see was him when I looked in the

mirror. I was judgmental. I was clueless about making a marriage work. My handwriting was just like his. And I was immersed in my own addictive behaviors.

At this point I had not spoken to him in over six years. I was blessed, though, that he and I lived long enough for me to get over myself and own the judgments I had placed on him. Long before his death, we were able to sit and talk as two men and gain some understanding of how each of us was shaped to become the men we were. I am forever indebted to him for his willingness and ability to be honest with me about his own limitations and truths.

In our last conversation he reinforced his love and understanding by apologizing for not being able to answer all of my questions. He knew those questions were important to me, and in his apology he took responsibility for the fact that it was his limitation that was in the way. This was his greatest act of love for me as a man.

A man who is stuck in his ego cannot be told anything and certainly is not open to learning. He is a lost boy who looks strong and tough on the outside yet on the inside is struggling with hurt and an overwhelming sense of smallness. There is one commonality in this condition: These men are incomplete with their fathers. We have legions of men who grew up with fathers who were absent, either physically or emotionally. The result is men with no defined purpose and with no access to the emotional tools they need to reach maturity.

All boys need to be guided into maturity; they need a sense of who they are becoming, what they will stand for, and what principles they should live by. Most fathers fail to realize that, through their example, they are at all times teaching their sons, and daughters for that matter, what an adult relationship with a woman looks like. They are modeling what it means to be a man. Many times men's behavior patterns with women mimic the inadequate patterns of their fathers. A father who is absent, whether physically or emotionally, leaves a deep void in his son's life. This void becomes the boy's own wound and subsequent journey to heal, and this healing can be done only with and through other men. Despite the enormous love a mother can have for her son, she cannot teach a boy how to become a man.

To create movement in your life, answer the following question:

When did you first consider yourself to be a man?

To gain a deeper understanding, please go to relationshipexcellence.com to post your thoughts and read responses from others who are also committed to creating relationship excellence.

Men's need for mentors

Every man needs a mentor: another man from whom he can learn what it means to be a man. Unfortunately, this has been lost in our society. As a result we see more and more men who are lost, wandering about with no means to communicate who they are and what they stand for. They have dug a huge hole for themselves and are stuck. They don't trust themselves or others. They end up going it alone, living shallow and painful lives, continuing an artificial story of what it means to be a man, and, based on that fallacy, trying to manipulate themselves into a world they know little about. They are unwilling to be transparent. They avoid being challenged, because they question their worth and fear losing their already shaky foothold on manhood. They must perpetuate their outward perception of what it is to be a man, at any cost.

The saying has not lost its truth: A man who lies with pigs becomes one. A man needs to evaluate the type of man he spends time with. Is he hanging out with men of integrity or with men who buy his bullshit and privately dismiss him? It is an important distinction. Is he willing to be challenged by other men and live life from a solid, principled place? Is he willing to live as an open book, to have the pages and chapters of his life scrutinized by men who will not hide behind fear of conflict, who will contribute honest and open feedback so he can live in his highest truth? He must be open to being influenced by the quality of relationships that would give his life meaning.

It is time for men to have this new awakening. How is it that men are natural born fixers and yet don't approach their relationship with this attitude of wanting to make things better? Men's typical relationship strategy today is throw away and replace. If a particular component of a relationship is flawed, or if their partner herself seems to be "broken," they move on; it is that simple. Men are so used to replacing the old, they've become lazy. They pay a big price for this carefree existence, however, because it truly seeps into various facets of their lives, including relationships.

Men think it infinitely more exciting to replace an old relationship than to try to repair the current one. The problem is, while a man may be thrilled with the novelty of the new, the same core issues remain, lying just beneath the surface.

Men's failure exists in not recognizing that until they change and evolve, they will recreate the same issues in any future relationship. A new relationship takes time, energy, and much effort to cultivate. They would be better served by using their efforts in their current relationship, looking at what they bring and how they could be different in order to create a different result.

Leadership

It is time for men to grow up and face the music. It is time for them to return to a way of being where they know what it is they stand for and are immovable in their stance in the world. Men are soft, so much so that the main attribute they neglect in a relationship is being taken up by women. That attribute is leadership. Men are failing to lead. They either go along with whatever women want or fight to keep them from having it. Because men are disconnected from what they want, they most often fight against the relationship instead of fighting for something in the relationship.

In fact, women today are better at being a man than most men are. They have been forced to fill men's shoes because men have decided not to take part. And men wonder why women trash them so much? They have only themselves to blame. I've heard it all. Men who claim they cannot be themselves because of the backlash from the modern woman. They believe women want men to be more sensitive and compassionate. What a tepid excuse for not being more of a man.

Men are afraid to say no to women, yet women want a man who is clear and confident, who knows what he wants. They lose respect for a man who doesn't say no. I'm not arguing that men should say no for the sake of saying no. I am calling for men to verbalize their stance clearly, from a clear and grounded place, without the fear of repercussion. I assure you that this, not tiptoe complacency, is what the relationship needs. I can tell you that one of the most common complaints I hear from women is that their husband won't say no. What happens? A woman's resentment carries over into the relationship and as a result she loses respect and faith in his ability to handle their security. Women want men to protect them, to look out for the well being of the whole family, emotionally as well as financially.

I know a man who planned to take his fiancée to an expensive restaurant for her birthday, three months prior to their wedding. It was her favorite restaurant. He knew she would love the experience. However, on the drive to the restaurant, he had a sinking feeling in his gut that he was about to make a big mistake. He knew he needed to honor that feeling. So he pulled over to the side of the road, took his woman's hands in his, and spoke his truth. Knowing that she had asked him to take care of their finances, he told her that spending $500 on dinner was not prudent, given the expenses they were committed to for their impending wedding. He told her he was going to cancel the reservation, drive to the supermarket, then take her home and cook her an amazing meal. Even though she was disappointed, she knew it was the right thing to do and their relationship was strengthened by it. Her trust had been reinforced. They could move forward, a stronger team. This is one aspect of leading in relationship that women want.

We test each other in relationships until we trust the other. Women test men until they are secure on two fronts. First, they want to trust a man to be a man, to protect them, and to set the tone for their family. And second, they want to be held in high regard and to be loved. Women respond powerfully to the experience of being loved. Much disconnection in relationships derives from the disparity between how men show love and how women perceive love. Men need love, too. They overcome challenges on the basis of love. They are inspired when their spouse admires them. For this to happen, men need to behave in a way that is admirable.

The feminine challenge

Because a woman picks her man, she will naturally challenge him to be his best. She will constantly test to see if he is truly being a great man and to see if he is committed to the relationship, to determine whether he is fulfilling his potential. She will continually challenge her man to be the best he can be. A man's response to testing demonstrates his strength of character. He may choose to perceive the testing as a complaint or as a compliment. If a man does not keep his word and is called on it and reacts with reasons, excuses, or childish anger in order to divert the conversation, his woman will see him as weak, living from a place of fear. She will eventually lose respect for him.

Many men aren't aware that throughout the animal kingdom, the feminine picks the masculine. When we get this as men, we can see the role we have played in the demise of the relationship: We haven't picked them back. Men need to realize that to be picked by a woman is a privilege, and that if he wants to be with her he needs to pick her back, fully.

Smart women let men think that they picked them. Certainly men are the ones who are supposed to get down on bended knee and ask their woman to marry them. This isn't enough. When a man truly picks back and joins with his woman as a team, her ongoing testing of him will diminish. A deep trust will develop between them that is palpable to the outside world.

When a woman asks her partner to take charge, to be the man, to do the right thing, the leader in him is being called into action. It isn't a sin for a man to not know how to step forward; it is a sin for him not to ask another man for support in doing so. True success happens in the world when men realize two things: Only they can do it, and they cannot do it alone. Asking for and receiving support is the key to accessing their own personal power.

Some truths about men

Men are bullshit factories. As alluded to at the beginning of this chapter, a man needs to have other men in his life who will hold him to his word and not accept his bullshit. Men who won't share honestly with other men on a regular basis remain rudderless on the waters of life. A man needs to face his fear in order to live from his truth. Without transparency in his life, a man will subvert himself, because he needs other men to both challenge him and champion him. This level of support helps him deepen his core emotional strength. When a man has friends who will hold his feet to the fire, his woman will encourage him to spend time with them. She gets a man who is more connected to himself, who has more self-confidence, and who better can connect with her.

Withholding his deeper truth from other men not only hurts a man, it also hurts all of his relationships. When men lack transparency in their lives, they cannot be fully supported to be the best they can be.

I once worked with a man who proudly told me of his friendship with three male friends from high school and of his two brothers. They regularly got together to stay connected. He was seeing me because his wife had found out he had been having an affair for five years and he wanted to restore his marriage. When I asked what feedback he had received from his friends about the affair, he disclosed that none of them knew. These were his best friends and none of them knew. How much depth can a relationship have if it lacks basic truths? If that man had been a friend of mine and had disclosed to me that he was even thinking of having an affair, I would have challenged him on his commitment to his marriage and his integrity.

Men often live by double standards. In fact, much of their anguish comes from this duality of thoughts. If a man is insecure and critical about the past sexual history of his partner, despite their own checkered past, she will see him as weak. There are men who think it cool to cheat; yet they would leave their wives for the same "indiscretion" on their part. Men will think it is all right for another man to cry, yet they would judge themselves as weak if they did so. The contradictions are endless.

Men can use anger as a cover for other emotions. They simply get angrier than the person in front of them to shut the other person down. They misunderstand the whole point of anger. Anger is a red flag that calls us to attention. It tells us that a boundary has been violated, that one needs to be established, and that we're feeling hopeless or helpless. Some men, when confronted with the truth, use anger as a defense mechanism. There is no greater way to lose other people's respect.

Men who live from their ego have a strong need to be right. Being right is an act of violence because others react strongly to being made wrong. A more subtle way of being right is to demand an apology. But apologies never need to be demanded. This is a subtle form of control. Apologies need to be freely offered from our own moral compass.

Men distract themselves with an affair or by pouring their energies into their work rather than being honest with their wives about what they need in the relationship.

A man who never answers the question at hand is trying to remain in control of the relationship. He fails to see that a relationship cannot be controlled. He is living through fear; that's why he stonewalls every conversation with phrases like "You do it, too" or "Why are you always picking on me?" or "You're lying; I don't believe you." A woman who is treated this way will lose respect for her man and choose to live a parallel and separate life.

Men need to learn not to make things personal and to not take things personally. When he makes everything around him personal as a father, the boy in him is in charge of the relationship. Boys don't raise children very well. The relationships will inevitably fail. Healthy parenting and marital relationships require the man to step up and establish healthy boundaries. This is where men need to grow up. Men can stop taking things personally when they are deeply connected to their core truths.

Men are naturally competitive. Women are naturally co-operative. There is an inherent problem with these two traits. For example, I often see men who are competing with their wives for their children's love. They crumble when their children tell him they don't like them and give in to the children's demands. When men give in, they place the structure of the whole family in great danger.

I have worked with men who refuse to see how having been sexually abused as a teenager is impacting their current life. They never open up and get close to other men. They become confused about how to set boundaries because theirs were violated. They don't trust other men or themselves. Until they deal with their wound, they will have no ability to form a deep, significant relationship.

Men who ignore the fact that their partners have been asking for change in the relationship will destroy those relationships through inaction. These men usually hear the requests or demands for change as criticism. This is how a man, yet again, gets in his own way. He is unable to see the big picture. In contrast, women are adept at seeing it. They are effectively able to see into the future of a relationship. They are often able to see the obvious signals of difficulties that lie ahead well before men do. In my experience it takes sudden loss or even death to wake men up. A man will most often be brought to his knees sobbing and pleading for a second chance when their woman finally decides to quit the relationship. At this point the man finally realizes that she had tried to bring focus to the relationship issue for so long and has given up. When men are willing to change only after such an event and solely to save the marriage, their attempt will usually fail. A man will evolve only when he is sick and tired of being the way he is and only because he wants to be a better man for himself first and then for the relationship. And a man has to choose to live through courage with an open heart or at minimum a bruised heart.

Men who make excuses and give reasons why they cannot do what they really want to do are refusing to face their fears and end up unfulfilled.

Most men do not know their purpose, do not know their direction, and are headed nowhere at a furious pace. They need to slow down, evaluate, and understand that a purpose needs to be bigger than their family, bigger than their job, and bigger than their goals.

The behavior of boys versus men

Most men are acting like boys trapped in the bodies of men. This is perhaps the quality women find most unappealing in men. A typical complaint of women is that their man is childish. The implications of this are nothing short of monumental, because of the ripple effect into every aspect of the relationship, in particular their sex life. Many of my sessions as a coach deal with this phenomenon. A woman is repulsed when her man is childish, and this throws off the relationship's sexual chemistry. A woman who is turned off in this way will not open up sexually.

In addition, a new dynamic is created, that of a mother-son relationship, in place of a husband and wife relationship. A woman perpetuates her man's behavior by acting like a mother to the "boy" in her man, which only reinforces the separation between the two. Neither boys nor men are interested in sleeping with "Mother energy." And when a man sulks after being turned down for sex, he perpetuates the disconnection. This is a place men need to grow through.

That said, it is critical for men to retain a sense of the boy. This energy is the origin of playfulness, fun, spontaneity, and adventure. One of the three things a man needs to be able to do is genuinely make his woman laugh. (See below for the other two.) But he must guard against allowing that boy to dictate the course of their relationship or more importantly to influence adult decisions. The boy can never be allowed to be in charge.

A woman knows the boy is in charge of their relationship when he behaves in any of the following ways:

- he lives perpetually in debt
- he keeps secrets
- he drives like a maniac with no regard for others on the road
- he holds grudges
- he keeps score
- he is juiced by drama and chaos
- he is unwilling to set boundaries with his own mother
- he needs to be right
- he is unable to apologize with sincerity
- he makes excuses
- he lives without vision
- he is invested in "looking good"
- he is afraid and unwilling to step up
- he complains and refuses to take action toward change
- he keeps the change when given more at a store
- he lies to male friends
- he thinks smoking pot on a daily basis is cool
- he stonewalls conversations with objections
- he buys a "toy" for himself without consultation or agreement in the family
- he will embellish the size of anything.

There are only two responses a woman needs to give a man when she experiences him as behaving like a boy in relationship:

1. That's so unattractive.

2. That's so not sexy.

I can guarantee that this will instantly spark in most men an opportunity for an awakening.

Here is how a man can succeed with a woman:

- by having a plan for his life and artfully communicating to his woman how he intends to bring it into being in the world
- by being able to make her laugh (the feminine can get overly serious)
- by meeting her both emotionally and sexually.

There is one response women typically feel when these needs are met: "That's so attractive."

To create movement in your life, answer the following question:

What is your biggest fear as a man?

To gain a deeper understanding, please go to relationshipexcellence.com to post your thoughts and read responses from others who are also committed to creating relationship excellence.

7

The Work of Women

*A woman should never please a man
just to change his mind*

WOMEN HAVE TO STOP MOTHERING men while complaining that they're behaving like boys.

Many girls were brought up as "daddy's little girl" or to be "the princess" — or if they weren't, they sure wanted to be. This is a normal and natural part of a girl's metamorphosis into womanhood. A girl's relationship with her father is potent. Her dynamic with her father significantly influences her views and expectations of men in adult relationships.

When a woman is incomplete with her father — when she hasn't established herself as a woman in his eyes — she is going to look for something from her boyfriend or husband that he's not going to be able to give her. Many adolescent girls who aren't able to navigate the transition they need into adulthood with their fathers develop a demanding attitude that ultimately pushes people away.

Women stuck in this emotional wound are often referred to as high maintenance. Others respond to the same situation by becoming meek and coquettish. They try to maintain the status quo by not placing high demands on a man. Whether high-maintenance or low-maintenance, these women are set up for disappointment.

The fear of transition

Women still have their work cut out for them. The women's movement has created a powerful opening for the co-creation with men of new relationship practices. The liberation from an archaic model of relationship is still under way and is far from complete. We're still stuck in the transition stage of this particular evolution. It is said that we're afraid of change. I think it is the in-between stage that we fear. Transition is more challenging to us than change. We get our feet on the ground only when we know for sure where we're headed. This transition requires couples to enter honest dialogue about masculine and feminine roles, essences, desires, and expectations to a degree unlike anything we have ever seen. Personal evolution has to happen if we are to survive our current relationship crisis. What is missing is the compelling factor that will see men and women join forces and co-create for the good of the whole, for the sake of the relationship.

As women have fought valiantly for equality, so much has been achieved, advancing humankind. Women have found their voices, which was necessary in order to create the change. They don't need men in the same way their mothers and grandmothers did. Many women are quite capable of taking care of themselves financially, of creating a family without a man present, of maintaining a property or dwelling. The roles of masculine and feminine and their archetypal energies have been blurred and obscured.

However, women have also lost something. In order to fit into the masculine-dominated world, they have had to develop their masculine energy. Many women have overdeveloped this energy to the point that they have become disconnected from their feminine essence. They have suffered painfully as a result. This rejection of their own femininity breeds an underlying distrust, bitterness, and resentment within them.

Traditional relationships were set up under a caretaking principle as opposed to a caregiving principle. When we are caretaking, we are essentially, as the word implies, taking something away from them through our care. Think about this. When one person handles the money in the relationship "because they are better at it," this disempowers the one not participating in the process. This is not to say that one of the couple shouldn't handle a specific area of the relationship. However, they need to involve the other in the process and share the knowledge and strategy that goes along with that area of the relationship. My parents had a traditional relationship in which my father was the breadwinner and my mother took care of the finances and ran the household. When my mother passed away, my father had no idea about taking care of bank accounts and his home. He was at some level disabled by the structure of the relationship.

Within the Relationship Revolution, both people need to support each other to be fully capable within the relationship and share strengths with each other. This way each will feel supported to become the best they can be. A relationship in which heavy caretaking is going on breeds either complacency or rebelliousness. Caregiving relationships look out for the best for both partners. In essence we are empowering the other to ask for support. We are requesting that they accurately describe for us what support looks like. In this way we can step in and support them in their greatness.

Yes, there is freedom for women in their newfound liberation. However, this freedom fails to address their core need to be paired with a partner in a deep, loving, committed, long-term relationship. Fundamentally, the feminine enters a relationship for security and protection. The true feminine essence wants to be cared for and looked after by the masculine. Yet men are on the sidelines watching, because they haven't caught up. They have no clue how to navigate this change because they have become confused regarding their role in face of the new relationship dynamics.

Women's lose-lose situation

The challenge we face as a society is that men are looking to women to guide them in what to do and in how to be. Women are in a lose-lose situation here. Although men ask them for direction, most of them will not take it because that would emasculate them. And women lose respect for men who do not take their direction.

Men are soft and need to regain their strength as men. Women want men to figure it out and decide for themselves who they need to be. This is not to say that men need to exclude the feminine; it is to say that they need to gather information from them and then decide from their own core what to say or do in any situation. Men need to figure their lives out in the company of other men. They need to be willing to fail and grow, getting up again and again as they traverse the gap between who they have been and who they are becoming.

A woman respects a man who can fail and recover, who can spill his guts and then clean it up.

As discussed earlier in this book, women at the beginning of a relationship ask for and accept too little from men. Once the relationship is established, they ask for too much. Men feel that women are being unreasonable. This becomes the beginning of relationship conflict. The secret is for us to start as we mean to go on. The strategy for asking for so little is one of the ways we have been taught to be indirect. This can be insidious, infecting the core of any relationship. We may have been punished for being direct in our childhood. Most of us learned well what works and what doesn't. And while this was a great way to survive childhood, it destroys our adult relationships. This is one of the ways we get in our own way.

The most powerful way to influence another person is to accept them exactly as they are. Accept your man as he is.

Regardless of our gender, we all want to be accepted. When we feel accepted, we can then receive feedback about how others experience us. This opens the space to gain an understanding of how it is we ended up this way. We have to get curious. Stop expecting your man to be something else. If your man's behavior is objectionable, and you have brought the impact of this to his attention, why are you still with him? Women need to understand that when they complain, men withdraw.

To create movement in your life, answer the following question:

What ways do you try to change your man even though you know from experience that they're not going to work?

To gain a deeper understanding, please go to relationshipexcellence.com to post your thoughts and read responses from others who are also committed to creating relationship excellence.

What women can share with men

The only thing women need to do is share with their man the impact of his behavior. "When you come home smelling of beer, I don't want to get close to you in that moment." Or "When you say you will do something and then you don't, it makes me lose trust in you." A woman's freedom is in observing him as he is and providing feedback in terms of his impact on her.

When she lives from an expectation that he will be different, she will be disappointed. When we're disappointed in someone, we often feel the need to change them in order to feel better ourselves. Our only other alternative is to withdraw. This becomes part of the relationship dance.

Compromise is both the great complaint and demand of the feminine. But when we compromise in relationship, both people give up what they truly want and "accept" less than what is desirable. And it isn't accepted if later we complain about having given it up. Consideration for the relationship is far more powerful than compromise. Consideration involves focusing on the needs of the relationship. What does the relationship need?

Think about consideration. What does it mean to be considerate? Without this quality, two people are competing for space in the relationship as opposed to working together to build something more powerful than the two of them. And if we don't know what we're working toward, we are working against it.

The "bitch"

I cannot believe it when women call themselves a "bitch." The term is disgusting. It is a setup for ridicule and oppression. Some women feel that when they have to put their foot down, when they mean what they say, when they need to make their point, they become a self-declared bitch. Given that we teach others how to treat us, it is no wonder that other men and women will throw the term back in their face.

Notice that the B word always has an edge to it; it is a strong putdown. This is one of the ways women derail themselves and set themselves up for self-hatred and judgment. An attitude will destroy a relationship. Whether it is one of "the princess" or "the entitled one" or "the bitch" or the one who "goes it alone," such attitudes are destructive to relationships.

The degree to which we trust ourselves is the degree to which we can trust another. Women have to learn to trust other women and create great friendships with each other. A woman's relationship with her mother sets the tone for all of her relationships with other women. A woman needs to accept the best in her mother and let the rest go. Some women fully connect with this energy only when they become a mother themselves.

Mother energy is powerful energy. Women have lost touch with their goddess energy and need to reclaim it. There is an expectation that women be polite, sweet, and accommodating. Women can be all these things and many more. The Earth is often referred to as Mother Earth because her energies are feminine. This energy is a powerful, radiant, creative force full of movement and vibrancy. The Earth is full of color, life, birth, and texture. Along with this powerful life force, Mother Earth also has many destructive energies: storms, tsunamis, hurricanes, and monsoons, as well as drought. All are necessary and encompass the fullness of range in the feminine.

It was William Congreve who said, "Hell hath no fury like a woman scorned." So true. The feminine longs to be met in this energy and it takes a man grounded in his warrior energy to meet her there. This is what the feminine is looking for: a man who won't be distracted by minutiae and who in his stillness can stand witness to the storm, loving the feminine fully as the storm passes through her. Many men are weak in this area and it is their growth edge to move through it and fully witness the depth of feminine emotion. Here a man will gain insight into the depth of her heart and will develop a deeper recognition of his own heart as well. This is when the relationship is truly being served.

A woman needs to accept a few things about a man. She needs to determine if eighty percent of him is satisfactory to her. If it is, then she should forgo the other twenty percent, putting it down to who he is.

I'm not asking women to overlook a man's lack of integrity or sense of honesty. I am asking them to look at whether or not they can love him as he is and accept him as the man he presents himself as being.

Women fall in love with the potential that a man can be in the world. She can see it. When a woman is in touch with her full potential, she won't settle for a man who has one foot on the dock and one foot in the boat of his own life or the relationship.

Try as she might, a woman cannot teach a man how to be a man. A mother cannot teach her son how to be a man. She needs to hand her sons at puberty over to her man so he can train them in the ways of being a man in the world. His job is to toughen them up to the challenges they will face. A woman needs to be celebrated for the work she has done in raising her children into adulthood.

To create movement in your life, answer the following question:

How have you taken your partner for granted in the past?

To gain a deeper understanding, please go to relationshipexcellence.com to post your thoughts and read responses from others who are also committed to creating relationship excellence.

8

The Work of Relationship

Relationships don't just happen; they're built

WE CREATE RELATIONSHIPS OUT OF our deepest longing to feel connected to each other. Our relationship is a dream that we have created. We fail to see that however painful or beautiful our relationship may be, we have dreamed it to be what it is. When we accept responsibility for this, individually or together, we can change any aspect of the relationship we desire.

We are powerful beings. Relationship excellence is a result not only of what we do but also of who we are being in relationship. We get to design and build the relationship we want.

As discussed earlier, our challenge is that our main model of relationship is from our family of origin, even though most of us would consider it flawed. When we join another in relationship, we bring with us the model of our family system. In the moment, while we're enraptured by the romantic and courtship phase of a relationship, we will talk openly of our dreams for an ideal relationship. We decide to join our lives out of the common threads we have identified in what we both want. Courtship is a playful experience; we learn about each other through play. As the relationship deepens, we are co-creating the relationship on the basis of, or in reaction to, our own faulty model. Even when we're reacting to this model, we're still operating from it. We create what we focus on.

Designing relationships

Relationships require work, and they are based on our dreams and imagination. Imagination is our least-used muscle. We lack the mental focus and discipline to stay with the picture of our dream relationship and bring it into reality. We have a felt sense in our body of our past but not of the future state we desire. Because we're emotionally driven and creatures of habit, we will reinvent, through unconscious behavior, the same feelings we had in the past. This is all we know for sure and we feel it is better to be with what we're sure of. We become lazy because we have few models of relationships that work. We fail to see that the way relationship unfolds is influenced by our unconscious behavior.

As a result, we avoid transparency on the journey of relationship. Trust is solely built on transparency. Families tend not to be transparent. Rules may include, "Don't tell your mother," "Don't tell," "We don't do that in our family,"

"What would the neighbors think?" There are always secrets in families.

A wonderful AA slogan says we're only as sick as our secrets. The only secrets worth keeping are ones that make us feel good. Imagine the liberation people would experience if their families were to teach this to them as children. We hide from each other because we haven't got it right yet, as if there is pressure to have arrived at a goal. We're afraid to tell the truth or ask for help because we feel that would mean we're weak. We don't know how to trust ourselves, so we don't know how to trust others. We wait to work on our relationship until it is in serious decline and we have created destructive or debilitating stories about ourselves and the other, as well as major distrust.

The only thing that's missing in any relationship is what we're not bringing to it. Rarely do we look at ourselves and ask, "What could I bring to the table that would change the direction of my relationship?" Our focus tends to be on the other and not on ourselves. We likely have a laundry list of things that our *partner* could do differently to make us feel better about the relationship. However, when we lodge a complaint in the relationship, we end up either implying that the other is wrong and needs to change or demanding that the other change.

The difference between a request and a demand is that when we make a request, yes, no, or counteroffers are all acceptable responses. When we ask a question and we don't like the response we get (we are triggered in some way), then what we asked was a demand couched as a question. Nobody likes to be told what to do. Nobody likes to be told what they need to do differently. The truth is, we know what we need to change in our lives in order to be happier and better adjusted.

As we take responsibility for creating the relationship we want, we will work from invitation. We have to step up ourselves and do our own work first.

When we're clear about what we want to change in ourselves, we get clear about what we're able to create. It all starts with us because we will now be able to start the process from a different place within ourselves.

Designing our relationship requires that we address the following factors:

- conflict
- imagination
- commitment.

Relationships and conflict

We get into conflict typically about the things we think and feel differently about. Conflict occurs when our needs aren't met. In this way, conflict is natural to relationship.

Consider the old saying, "If two men in business always agree, one is unnecessary." We all want to be seen and accepted for who we are. We want our perspective to be seen and heard. We want our partner to see how our perspective might contribute to the betterment of the relationship. The differences between us are often apparent. Just think of how siblings, brought up in the "same family," have such different ways of seeing the world. We all see our parents, our family, and ourselves differently. The differences stem from our perspectives.

The work of relationship requires tolerance for each other's perceptions. Curiosity and fascination are essential here. Conflict arises when we're attached to others seeing the world through our lens — when we're attached to their agreement with our view of reality. Think about how three people sitting in the same room will have different views of the room depending on where they are sitting. They will have different objects in their sight lines. Their perception will be influenced as well by their individual preference for color, texture, lighting, form, and function. And yet they are all in the same room.

People who want to create a successful business have to work *on* their business and not be trapped by working *in* their business. This is why major corporations have people whose main function is to present differing views in order to stimulate growth and maximize the potential of the group. Working on the business is particularly challenging for the self-employed. Often they are the chief cook and bottle washer, so they fail to work on creating the freedom they originally longed for when they embarked on their business. A business needs to support the lifestyle of the people working in it.

Similarly, most people work *in* their relationship, not *on* it. The value of working on the relationship is the immediate separation that occurs. It is as if we get to stand on a chair and look down more objectively on the events unfolding in the relationship.

Einstein's insight, quoted earlier, comes into play here: "You cannot solve a problem from the same consciousness that created it." Elevating the consciousness of our relationship creates insight into what the relationship needs. From here we can actually design an alliance that moves away from the typical problem-solving conversations into designing what works. Problem solving never works because the focus is on the problem and most people end up feeling criticized in that context. This is a major shutdown area in relationship for most people — especially men. Whatever we focus on is what grows.

Since many people are conflict averse, they hope things will somehow get better rather than reframing conflict as growth trying to happen.

There are five underlying causes of all arguments and conflicts in relationship.

1. Our deep need to feel acknowledged

What happens if we feel we're not seen or heard, whether it is about cleaning up the yard, doing the laundry, or bringing home a paycheck? Rather than ask directly for acknowledgment, we argue about something that irritates us or sends us over the edge. There is a deep vulnerability in asking for what we want. Most of us have been trained, one way or the other, not to do so. I recall as a child being told to "quit wanting — you're always want-ing something!" Yet when we are acknowledged for our contribution, be it to a conversation, to cleaning up the house, or for a thoughtful action, it lands in us powerfully.

2. Our deep need to be celebrated

Being celebrated is a knife-edge. We long to experience being celebrated for exactly who we are in any given moment, yet at the same time we push such a compliment away. Notice what comes up inside you as you read the following sentences — these feelings are a clue to under-standing yourself. Imagine yourself seated at a banquet along with a thousand other guests. Someone you know and love is making their way up to the podium to give a twenty-minute speech acknowledging and celebrating you. What would you want them to say?

Recall an experience when you were the center of attention and felt uncomfortable about it, or conversely a time when a special occasion went by and people impor-tant to you didn't go the distance in celebrating you.

3. Our deep need to be heard

Being heard is different from being listened to. People will complain to someone that they aren't listening and will receive the retort that they *are* listening. Listening to the words is one thing. When we really hear another person, we are actively engaged in hearing the deeper meaning they are conveying. When we care about the speaker and the circumstance enough to listen with all of our senses, we pick up the subtle meaning and intent in their words. It is an act of love to offer this gift to another. We know deep within us when another person has heard us in this way. When we are truly heard, it is as if nothing else needs to be spoken and we can rest peacefully.

From this place of feeling truly heard and met — where we feel witnessed and understood by another — we can let go of old pain and hurt. This ability to read the subtext in a conversation, or the bigger context of the conversation, is an essential skill to be learned in the Relationship Revolution.

4. Our deep need to be validated

To validate another is to establish their truthfulness or soundness. This is different from agreeing with them. Validation is a process of authenticity and confirmation. We can validate a person's goodness or generosity or impact on others.

It is rare for us to receive this kind of feedback. The strong reaction we feel when we receive validation or acknowledgement, whether publicly or privately, is ours to work through. When we deflect a compliment or acknowledgment because of our own discomfort, we are being disrespectful to the person giving it. Most people enjoy the act of giving but have a hard time with receiving. Yet, when we refuse to accept another's compliment with gratitude and grace, we are robbing that person of the pleasure of giving.

5. Our deep need for personal space

An important part of dealing with conflict in relationship is achieving different degrees of alone time verses together time. Sometimes the need for alone time is the result of stress in our life — "where we're at" in our life — as well as of personal and individual needs. Introverts, for example, need more alone time than do extroverts.

If couples lack a successful way to negotiate alone time versus together time, an argument will blow up to *create* space away from each other. If asking for alone time is perceived as a threat to the relationship, the only way to successfully create it is to argue and to go off into separate corners. This is an indirect and destructive way to nurture our need to regroup and reconnect within ourselves.

The old saying that "absence makes the heart grow fonder" underscores something important about keeping excitement alive in a relationship. I know several relationships that work well because both partners in the relationship have negotiated at least one separate vacation per year. They both look forward to their reunions and celebrate what they value in their reconnection.

Some people argue as a way of connecting and staying engaged. There are couples and indeed families whose identity is built by moving from crisis to crisis. Conflict is what holds them together. A crisis gives them "an excuse" for intimacy and connection.

We humans have the most amazing capacity to take another person or situation for granted. We have all felt taken for granted at some point in our lives. Our reaction to this experience points us to our deeper longing for feeling acknowledged, validated, heard, or celebrated. As we design our relationship, we have to choose to bring this level of focus to the meaning and opportunity that conflict brings.

One of the easiest ways to resolve taking another for granted is through the following exercise. Find three things a day that you can acknowledge your partner for and be creative in the ways you let them know. Small things that matter and make a difference in your life. Remember, while the pain of life is in the details, so is the pleasure.

Relationships and imagination

In creating relationship excellence with another, we need to focus on what we truly want. When I ask people this question, the most common answer I receive is, "I don't know." The next most common is, "What I *don't* want is ..." These answers are a start, but they are still an avoidance of our deepest truth. We know what we want and are afraid to ask for it because we know it will require energy and focus. We will have to accept responsibility for bringing the dream into reality. We have become lazy and stuck in instant gratification, content to live shallow, unfulfilled lives.

Are you willing to work for what you want? Are you willing to step up and be the source of your own creative power? It takes imagination.

Another gambit people take is to admit to themselves what they want and then make up stories about why they could never have it. They downgrade their desires to a more "acceptable level" of what they think is possible for them. Such people need to understand that two people can co-create whatever they truly desire in this world. Working together on vision and connection is worth it.

Designing our relationship goes completely against the notion that relationships are just supposed to happen. We fall in love and feel great about each other. But if all it took were love, we wouldn't have such high rates of strife and divorce. I have heard this statement a thousand times: "If we have to work this hard on the relationship, then it's not the right one." In most instances, nothing could be further from the truth. It takes two to make a relationship work. It also takes two to destroy it. We have to learn how to get out of our own way and open ourselves to a natural flow in relationship.

Think of your relationship as two people creating and caring for a garden. Both of you get to determine the size and shape of the garden. You get to decide which flowers blossom in your garden. Gardens need to be attended to. They need sunlight and shade. They go through seasons and have a different look and feel as they weather the elements that each season brings. There are dry spells and droughts, and at times downpours as well.

From time to time all gardens need to be weeded. Weeds can also be composed back into the garden. When two people attend to the garden in a loving way, it flourishes and provides an environment where it is pleasant to hang out.

All relationships generate manure. Most people take flowers (wonderful experiences) and turn them into shit. It is better to plant the flowers in manure (the shit of life) and benefit from their blossoming.

The French philosopher Michel Onfray says that when we first meet someone we are nothing to each other. From nothing we become everything and once we become everything we again become nothing.

This is the choice point where many people let the relationship fall apart. But this is where the relationship can go deeper, where we can co-create from a deeper love. This is a place where we get to hang out in the tension that is a natural part of relating. Rich learning is available to us here, if we're willing.

From the standpoint of being nothing, we are excited to discover who this person is. We spend lots of time looking into each other's eyes and drinking in the discovery of who they are. Our imaginations are on over-drive as we picture whether we could be together. As the relationship deepens, we may have the experience of falling in love, which is often described as romantic love. This is a natural and necessary stage. Without romantic love we would rarely join with another.

At this point we usually fall into the trap of becoming everything to each other. This state is both magical and oppressive. We can feel overwhelmed by having to be the all that the other expects us to be, the one who makes them happy. Or we may feel overwhelmed by the internal pressure of what we expect ourselves to be. The pressure of being everything prompts us to withdraw and pull away. In the confusion that arises at this stage, we lose ourselves. All of a sudden we don't know who we are anymore. We become afraid and withdraw, either making the other nothing or becoming the nothing ourselves.

This is the crisis line in relationship, the point where we decide if we will go deeper into and through our own fears and co-create a connection rooted in self-respect, in seeing ourselves and the other as creative, resourceful, and whole.

Most people think there are three possible outcomes.

There is the probable outcome: what will happen as long as things stay the same as they are right now. This is an illusion, because things only ever get better or worse. The law of the universe tells us that everything is the world is either growing and evolving or dying and decaying.

There is the catastrophic outcome: what will happen if things in the relationship continue to escalate and devolve the way they are right now. This is most likely to happen for those who have yet to rein in their resistance to the impact of their own behavior.

Finally there is the desired future or outcome: where we actively enroll our imagination and will to create the image in our mind of the future we truly want. Since the future exists only in language, we have a responsibility to put that image powerfully into words. As we do so, the words act as a magnet that draws us forth to the reality expressed. To be part of the Relationship Revolution requires us to be willing to go this distance, especially since the consequences of not doing so have been devastating for us in the past.

Any couple, or family for that matter, needs to regularly re-vision their desired outcome. We need to take into account life events, births, marriages, deaths, and ill health, to name a few, as we evolve through these life experiences. Even though I was complete with my parents individually and quite prepared for their death, nothing could have prepared me for the reality of the impact their deaths had on my view of my life. Without question it was a time of review and re-visioning. It doesn't matter how many books we read, whether about childbirth, parenting, or death, nothing brings us into reality like the actual experience.

To support you in co-creating a vision and for a free download of The Relationship Revolution Revisioning chart, go to relationshipexcellence.com.

To create movement in your life, answer the following question:

What five things would you like to change about yourself that would have you be more content?

To gain a deeper understanding, please go to relationshipexcellence.com to post your thoughts and read responses from others who are also committed to creating relationship excellence.

Relationships and commitment

An essential step in relationship is to examine whether we're willing to commit to changes that will better the relationship. After all, it is our happiness that is on the line. Committing requires us to go above and beyond doing what we currently know how to do and do whatever needs to be done. It is a move up to doing whatever it takes in our own lives.

Committing also requires us to get support. True support happens only when we declare our goal to another and specifically ask them to support us. We have to be specific about what support looks like to us and enroll them in supporting us in a way that works for us. This, too, is a process that needs to be revised from time to time.

Supporting the other in their goals is just as critical for relationship excellence as asking that we be supported in ours. This is an area of vulnerability. Most people are afraid to be told no and take themselves out of the game before even asking. This is another example of how we create and live from story or illusion.

Sometimes we step in and support someone else even though they haven't asked us. This is meddling, not support. It is based on our agenda of what we think they need. We will always miss the mark when we do this and most likely end up feeling unappreciated or taken for granted in the relationship. That's what happens when we do things without the other requesting it of us. We must stop that!

Let's say you discover that you really want to work in another country and you bring this truth to your partner. This is likely to initiate conflict. If it doesn't align with your partner's idea of being together, it will be seen as a threat to the relationship. You are likely going to experience pushback, resistance, and conflict. The question is, how do we support the other to have what it is they want when it is contrary to what we want?

This kind of situation is challenging and stretches us to look at what we're committed to and what we're attached to in the relationship. Are we in the relationship to have the other do what we want them to do in order to make us happy? Or do we want them to be happy in the world, sharing their joy from that place?

We have all shared certain life experiences, which have impacted us differently. At some level and to different degrees we have all felt betrayed, hurt, and abandoned. We have been lied to, have lied to others, have been wrongly accused, and have been punished whether we were at fault or not. We have felt humiliated and ashamed and, knowingly or not, have all humiliated and shamed others. We have been embarrassed and judged; we have felt controlled and inhibited. These are part of the range of experiences through which we grow up. And whether we realize it or not, all of these experiences support and shape us in becoming fully human. For some of us, our emotional development may have been arrested by painful or traumatic experiences.

At any point in an interaction with another we may be triggered into a past pain associated with one of these experiences. At such a point we may be so uncomfortable with the tension in our bodies that we want to leave in order to relieve that tension. Running at the first sense of such tension may have become a habit for us.

We are good at leaving. Staying is another matter. In order to stay in the tension, we have to take responsibility for the experience in our body and own it. If the tension or trigger is strong to the point that it overwhelms us, we may need to leave the room to collect ourselves; in such a case we have a responsibility to acknowledge our desire to leave, telling our partner that we will be back. We need to give a time frame for our return and keep to it. Failure to do so will inevitably trigger any abandonment issues in our partner.

So we may need to leave the room to gain a better perspective of what is going on for ourselves and the other. We may actually need to leave the building and go for a walk or a drive (not recommended when we are triggered). Upon our return, within the time frame we have committed to, we need to be able to tell our partner in responsible language (without blame) what was and is going on in us.

When we have something to say to another, we have a responsibility to set the tone for the communication. This involves asking for what we want in order to increase our chances of success.

When we talk to another, we have different needs than they do. It is the responsibility of the communicator to ask the receiver if they would be willing to listen in that moment. We may need to vent or even whine for five minutes. We may want feedback; we may not. Most often we can work things through simply by having a forum in which to speak. We may be looking for solutions to be listed and may want validation of our experience. We may simply want the experience of another hearing us. Being direct and up front with our partner sets out the expectations clearly.

Three powerful acts of service

There are three powerful acts of service that we can offer in any relationship.

The first is to find out what the other person wants and give it to them. This is true in all relationships. Why are we afraid of asking what the other wants? Could it be the fear of discovering that they don't want to be with us or that we cannot give them what they want? That we are somehow inadequate? Could it be that we're afraid to ask for what *we* truly want?

We need to bring the fears we're feeling to the surface so we can deal with them and let them go. Failing to do so will cause our fears to run the relationship and therefore our life. In its truest sense relationship is a vehicle designed to serve us so we can evolve in this way. Its very purpose is to enable both members of a relationship to experience life in its fullness. That includes what we might label as "good, bad, and indifferent."

The second act of service we can offer is to explore what commitment means to each of us together. In this process we have to make commitments to a particular set of outcomes. In our culture we believe men are commitment phobic. This is a myth and a destructive one at that. As mentioned earlier, none of us actually has difficulty with commitment. What we have in our lives right now is what we're committed to. Think about it: We must have been committed to the results we have or they wouldn't be manifest in our lives right now. Our failure is in not understanding that we are always at choice. It is *what we choose* that needs to change if we want something new.

Are you committed to connection or disconnection? The results speak for themselves. Are you committed to concealing or revealing? Again, look at the results. Have you ever deliberately set out to hurt your partner? Have they felt hurt in the relationship? I imagine that the answer to the first question is no and to the second, yes. If this is so, then what we're dealing with are misperceptions.

However, if you have set out to hurt your partner, then why would you or they stay in a relationship that includes a deliberate intent to hurt? After fifteen years of coaching couples, I can count on one hand the cases in which people have intentionally set out to hurt their partner. This includes relationships where infidelity has occurred.

I marvel at our capacity to be so unconscious in the moment as to imagine that our behavior will go unnoticed and therefore not affect the other.

This leads us to the third and most precious act of service in all relationships: to tell the truth to each other. When we're willing to live in courage and be with our truth, radical shifts will take place in our lives. Truth is an interesting phenomenon to explore. You see, truth is often what we believe it to be. We cannot change anything in our lives until we're willing to tell the truth about it. This requires us to reach deep inside and question what is in fact true for us and how that truth was determined. The degree to which we can do this is ultimately the degree to which we can get out of our own way.

We all want connection. That's essentially what this book is about: the authentic creation of connection and more specifically what we put in its way.

Rules of engagement

We turn now to Rules of Engagement, which are structures and agreements that support authentic connection. Many couples make the agreement to live inside a monogamous relationship. This for many people is a crucial agreement that can be tested daily. When we understand truth, impact, respect, and trust and we find ourselves challenged about fidelity, it becomes a no-brainer that the agreement trumps a momentary desire.

Furthermore, the rules of engagement that we create, personal as they are, will hold us steadfast on our course in the deepest moments of our relationship. These non-negotiables become the cornerstones of how we conduct ourselves in the structure of the relationship.

The rules of engagement in a relationship are the structures for working through whatever comes up in the relationship. There is a saying in the book *A Course in Miracles* that love brings out everything unlike itself. This is so, first, because only in the presence of love (acceptance) is it safe for us to reveal ourselves, and, second, because only in its presence can the wounds that we bring from our past be healed.

We need to understand that love is a choice. We choose to love another. When we attempt to close our hearts, we stop love from flowing in both directions. We are at choice here and it is the most powerful one we have: to close down our hearts or open up our hearts. Closing our hearts causes a slow death. It may feel that we are dying when we live with an open heart, because our heart will from time to time become shattered. However, a wounded heart is an opportunity to live fully. It is here that we know we are fully alive.

When we choose to open our hearts, a palpable shift is felt at the very center of our chest.

We get to design our rules of engagement in relationship. The question we need to answer is, "What does the relationship need for it to flourish?" Answers to this question may initially be informed by what we don't want or have suffered through in the past. However, while each relationship is as unique in its design as the participants in it, there are some common needs that serve most relationships well. Rules of engagement are the agreements we make together that take into consideration the needs of both and serve to enrich the relationship. That we hold our agreements sacred is more important than the actual content of our agreements. When we hold an agreement in high regard, it calls us forth into being the best we can be.

Let's look at some key rules of engagement.

Rule #1: We will not allow any threats to the relationship

As mentioned earlier, as a small child I experienced my mother's frustration with my father and her threats to leave him. I was afraid she might not take me with her. Later on in my life, as I was learning about myself in relationships, I panicked if a partner threatened to leave me. My reaction was that of a seven year old whose security was threatened.

We can always tell when we're triggered because two things happen. First, the reaction to the actual event is greater than warranted. Second, our behavior becomes juvenile and fearful. Being triggered is actually a good thing. We need to take responsibility for the trigger. Healing is required here. Only compassion from others and curiosity from ourselves will help close the wound. Anything else is simply a band-aid that will soon wash off.

Sometimes the person triggered will go into controlling behavior and tell the other how they have to be in order for them to feel safe. This is not going to create healing. In fact it makes things worse because it will trigger the feeling of being controlled. Nobody likes being told what to do. It takes us right back to childhood.

For a couple to feel safe and open, they need to agree that they will stay in the process until both feel good. If the relationship is under the threat of one person leaving, then there is no basis for growing through things together. We may need to examine the fear that would stand in the way of making such a commitment. My partner's favorite phrase when we get disconnected is, "Well, you're stuck with me." I have to admit that I love hearing this, because it means to me that no matter how hard it gets, we're going to work it through.

Rule #2: We will be fully present for important communications

Don't attempt to say anything important while either of you is engaged in an activity. When one of you is washing up after dinner or changing the baby — these are not the times to talk about the fact that you received a written warning at work. Worse still is trying to talk about an important issue while the other is driving.

Negotiate a time to talk when both of you are able to be fully present. Sit facing each other and have some physical contact. No couple can solve any problem unless they have a physical connection. Touch reminds us that we're on the same team. Anger is unlikely to escalate when we're engaged in loving, reassuring contact with each other.

It is also important to start the conversation with the end goal in mind. Perhaps you want to stay connected while you share some painful information and you just want your partner to hear you. Perhaps you are fearful and need some reassurance that you will get through this challenge together.

Ask for what you want. The key here is to get close when you have the desire to move away and create distance. You are on the same team. We resolve life's challenges together, not separately. A powerful construct is for a man to consciously hold his partner for twenty minutes a day. This is non-sexual safe holding. If a couple is willing to enfold each other in this deliberate way on a daily basis, the relationship will deepen in a profound way. Such couples will have the felt sense of being on the same team; they will be able to open up their deeper feelings and truths and share what's going on for them.

Rule #3: We will acknowledge and build on our communication

When we acknowledge something that's important to our partner, we are focusing on and validating the outcome desired. In this context, there are a few structures that couples need to look out for and change, including:

Black and white thinking

When we're stuck in "all or nothing" thinking, there's no room for possibility. We won't feel heard if we focus on extremes. Think about it, even in a black-and-white photograph, there is little actual black or white. The photograph is primarily made up of shades of gray.

Blaming, defending, protecting, or justifying

When we're caught in any of these behaviors, we are hooked; we are taking things personally. We have lost our objectivity. Communication in a relationship is about the relationship, not about us individually.

Rule #4: We will live from invitation

Our work in relationship is to ask for what we want. From there we continue to invite the other into a space of possibility. This requires us to be grounded in our own gifts and talents. It requires us to know our strengths and what we're committed to being in the moment. This way we aren't sidetracked by the drama and chaos; we stay on course.

Rule #5: We will create an environment for telling the truth

To flourish, a relationship needs truth. When we agree to tell the truth, we get to discover and uncover deeper parts of ourselves. (See more about this in the following chapter.)

You may also create agreements about what you will do if you get stuck in your communication and need third-party support. About the use of strong language, how anger will be supported, and so on. My partner and I have an agreement that neither of us will swear at the other. You choose the agreements that work best in supporting your relationship dream and vision.

These rules of engagement form the non-negotiables of relationship. They are the codes of conduct to abide by as a family. Whether your family numbers two or twelve, these are the principles that will bring alignment and focus to your lives. Principles you can count on and return to when you get off course.

To create movement in your life, answer the following question:

What are the non-negotiables in your relationship?

To gain a deeper understanding, please go to relationshipexcellence.com to post your thoughts and read responses from others who are also committed to creating relationship excellence.

9

Telling the Truth

The truth will set you free,
but first it will make you miserable

THE TRUTH, THE WHOLE TRUTH, and nothing but the truth? You mean I have to tell the truth?

We cannot change anything in our life until we tell the truth about it. We are all capable of telling the truth. It is completely up to us whether we do so or not. We know our truth. Only we can stop ourselves from speaking it. Most people seem to think they would be unable to maintain relationship in the real world if they spoke their truth. Just the opposite is the case: We cannot maintain a relationship unless we tell the truth. And the truth can be frightening because it can and will change us as well as the circumstances in our lives.

Truths about relationship truth

We are hungry for the truth. Our obsession with live talk shows and reality shows on television is based in our deep-seated hunger to know the truth. What is this celebrity really like? How will this person react under pressure? We long to know whether they are the same as we are and if we can even relate to them. Deep within us, we know that connection can happen only through truth.

It isn't fashionable to tell the truth — perhaps it never was. History is replete with examples of people who have paid the price for telling the truth. Is this the cause of our deep-seated fear of truth? We're willing to lie to ourselves and others under the guise of political correctness and social norms. This only serves to kill our vitality. Lying deadens us. We justify our withholding of the truth and our lying by telling ourselves we're protecting others from feeling bad about things. This is arrogant because it assumes that others are too weak to handle the truth. The deeper truth is that we are afraid of our own truth, deeper feelings, and power.

The truth is powerful and at times unpopular. The truth is vital if we are to live full out. The world needs it and so do our relationships. The Relationship Revolution is built on our core desire to live in truth. Until a couple, a family, an organization, or a country decides to live this way, all we can hope for is more of the same small-minded and fearful ways of interacting.

The truth is an evolving process. Our truth when we were twenty and our truth today will be vastly different. The trouble is, in the moment we think, "That's it. That's the truth!" In the moment, we take it personally and instantly create a story about what "the truth" means for the long term. Have we forgotten that truth is a moment-to-moment thing? Are we so addicted to telling ourselves we need to know the future that we make up the story in order to have some certainty about it?

Whenever we make up a story, it is an illusion. And when we make up stories, we mostly tell ourselves a catastrophic ending. No wonder we live from fear. Parents whose teenagers leave the nest often have a hard time with the truth that their children have grown up and left home. They need to accept that their kids need to find their own path. When I was thirty my parents still saw me as the sixteen year old who had left home. They were suffering from relationship jet lag: They still hadn't adjusted to me as a grown-up who was alive and well in the world.

Some people see themselves as having no problem speaking the truth — it is just that most people cannot handle what they say. They tell the truth all the time, liberally. My experience is that these people tell their truth from a place of anger. People have trouble hearing them not because they're afraid of the truth but because they feel disrespected.

When we choose to tell the truth, we need to do so with an open and loving heart. The way to tell truth from a place of love is to share from our experience and therefore without judgment. Think about it. "I feel hurt as a result of you lying to me about the affair" is completely different from, "You're nothing but a liar and a cheat." When we're talking about another, we're more likely to embellish, distort, and accuse. When we're talking about ourselves and our experience, it is easier and preferable to speak the truth.

Telling the truth in relationship takes a willingness to be vulnerable. It takes courage. We are in a constant process of discovering what the truth is for us. The truth is inarguable. When we talk about our own truth, no one can tell us it isn't so. When we talk about (and judge) others, we are lining ourselves up for arguments.

As we explore truth telling, it is as important to examine why we avoid telling the truth. What are the barriers to truth telling? What causes us to lie so obviously? In the example above, rather than be angry that a person has lied, we could ask ourselves if we have made it safe for them to tell the truth.

Learning to tell the truth after many years or maybe decades of not doing so can be painful. However, not telling the truth is also a very painful way to live. We can deceive ourselves to the point that we believe our own lies.

Denial is different. At some time or another we have all been in denial and we may still be in certain areas of our life. Denial is a necessary part of maturing and growing up. We deny something when we aren't ready to deal with it. There is a healthy and necessary side to denial. We need to feel supported and accepted if we are to face what we're in denial about.

When the writing is on the wall, read it! So often something important can be glaring right at us and we cannot see it because we're not ready to face it. You may be dating a guy and the first time you go over to his place, you see that his place is a disaster. He may or may not be embarrassed about this, but you decide he'll change if you love him enough — or worse still if he loves you enough. Or somehow you overlook the fact that your date is rude to waiters. Tell yourself, and them, the truth.

We don't read that writing on the wall because it calls us forth into our truth. A person I know once willfully damaged an item in a store when we were out shopping. I quickly realized that the anger I felt was linked not only to the act but also to my powerlessness to stop it. I told this person how I felt. I asked her to take responsibility for her actions and compensate the store for the damaged article. If I had failed to notice, face, and determine the truth, and to speak up and set the tone for how I wanted the relationship to be, the relationship would have failed.

Most of us have had the experience of telling the truth and not being appreciated for doing so. We may have even been punished for it. We may even have been wrongly accused and not been believed when we told the truth. These experiences from our past are painful and shape how we respond in the present and going forward.

As children growing up, we may have been punished by a parent for lying. We may also have observed that there were lies and secrets between our parents. So we were confused when we were punished for doing the same thing as they. What lesson did we learn from the experience? Most likely we became better at lying. So good that we rarely if ever got caught.

Lying is exhausting and creates withdrawal from the relationship. Our energy becomes invested in the concealment of the truth. We're afraid that the truth will spill out of us if we aren't on our toes. The less we say, the safer we are. However, we cannot change anything in our lives until we tell the truth about it, first to ourselves and then to others.

One of life's ironies is that we cannot get to the truth within us except by speaking openly with another. We need openness in dialogue to discover our truth. Unfolding the truth is a process of discovery that happens when we're willing to risk not knowing and to open up into the space of knowing. This is risky. We need the safety in a relationship to explore our "current reality" with the view that it might change. There is no place for judgment here. Judgment shuts down all levels of safety and bumps up against our own internal critic. We have all felt the pain of judgment. Judgment serves to imprison us. We become slaves to the judgment and withdraw and hide.

The openness required in unfolding the truth can be achieved only in the spirit of curiosity — the kind a seven year old has. We need to become fascinated with what might be true for us. In this exploration of ourselves, we get to look at who we really are, what we believe, where those beliefs originated from, and what truly matters — and then to live from internal peace. This happens only from a place where there is a high degree of trust.

Truth telling can be quite disconcerting. For some couples this is the fracture point. The vulnerability felt at this point could send the relationship toward greater health or put it on the path of danger. We're always at choice.

The greatest act of service we can offer another human being is to tell them the truth, the whole truth, and nothing but the truth. When we see telling the truth as an act of service to the relationship, magic happens.

> To create movement in your life, answer the following question:
>
> **What truth would you share in your relationship if you felt free to do so?**
>
> To gain a deeper understanding, please go to relationshipexcellence.com to post your thoughts and read responses from others who are also committed to creating relationship excellence.

Half truths

We can sense when the information we have is incomplete. We need to take time and slow down enough to detect the signals that we have been told a half-truth or that parts of a conversation are being left out. Sometimes we may simply have a nagging feeling that something isn't right. At other times, like a splash of cold water in our face, we know. When we experience a half-truth, we may judge the person or make up a story to "fill in the blanks" or both.

What we make up and tell ourselves is often much worse than any truth could be. Think of a time when a loved one didn't return home on time. Our imagination runs wild. We make up a story. It isn't fact; it is an illusion filled with interpretation, usually with a tragic ending. Imagine taking the same information and making up five entirely different stories with either happy or sad endings. None of the scenarios is real.

Why do we do this? Because we're used to feeling bad about things? Because the brain simply likes to create catastrophic events? Or is it an indication of just how firmly we live in the grip of fear and distrust?

To create movement in your life, answer the following question:

> What have you been unwilling to tell the truth about in relationship and what has prevented you from doing so?

To gain a deeper understanding, please go to relationshipexcellence.com to post your thoughts and read responses from others who are also committed to creating relationship excellence.

Is tolerance a virtue?

We need to cultivate tolerance. However, tolerating what we cannot handle or don't like in a relationship breeds resentment. We need to use our response or reaction to something as a way to understand ourselves, our limitations, and the choices we face.

When to tell the truth

Believe it or not, a whole lot of lying and withholding goes on during the early stages of courtship and dating. If we're interested in the other, we put on our best face. And we look for what we want to see in the other. We refuse to read the writing on the wall and tell ourselves the truth about our experience; we won't risk challenging the other about their behaviors and intentions. If we fear conflict, as most people do to some degree, we will overlook important facts and factors about the experience we're having.

If only we had the courage to start as we mean to go on. If only we had the ability to not take another person's behaviors personally. If our moral principles were firmly embedded within, we would take the risk of being vulnerable. In this way we could set the tone for the relationship we truly want.

Early in a relationship, we attach all kinds of meaning to the other person's behavior without checking the reality with them. We do and say so many things in order to look good and be accepted. This is deception in its most subtle form.

We do not intentionally go into this deceptive place when we're dating. The desire to get what we long for, the unconscious fear we have of rejection and not being good enough — these can, and will, make trouble for us in the relationship. It bears repeating: In the beginning we ask for too little in order to be accepted, then as the relationship deepens we ask for too much. The contrast between the two experiences brings confusion and conflict. Our need to be liked causes us not to be ourselves and consequently we don't like ourselves.

I believe we are all essentially good. I don't believe people are bad or ever intend to be. In fact we may be struggling with self-esteem and the perception of whether or not we can tell the truth.

What if we saw relationship as an invitation to join in the discovery of our own truth? We truly get to know ourselves only in relationship. Sitting at home alone won't get us very far down the path of self-discovery.

Part of the design of any relationship needs to include agreements about truth telling. This can happen only when there is a conscious agreement about how the environment will be created. When the conscious agreement is in place to tell the truth, we get to uncover and discover deeper parts of ourselves. This opens up more choice and freedom in the relationship.

To create movement in your life, answer the following question:

What truth is the most challenging for you to acknowledge?

To gain a deeper understanding, please go to relationshipexcellence.com to post your thoughts and read responses from others who are also committed to creating relationship excellence.

10

Three Relationship Builders

To heal the world, we must first heal ourselves

UNTIL WE BECOME AWARE THAT WE are the ones in our own way in relationship, we won't be able to shift our perspective. We create our outer world from what is within us. So when we change our inner landscape, our outer world changes.

I have found that couples experience major growth when they tap into the three major relationship builders of admiration, trust, and respect.

Admiration

ad·mire
1. to regard somebody or something with a feeling of pleasure, approval, and, often, wonder
2. to have a high opinion of somebody or something, for example, a quality or attribute

Have you ever stopped to wonder why it is so hard for some people to love themselves? People seem to have such difficulty with self-love. How did we get so disconnected from our essence? What happened? What could we have possibly done to deserve the self-loathing, self-hatred, and harshness we wield against ourselves?

Most people can come up with a litany of things they don't like about themselves. I often bring to people's attention the vast difference between who we are and what we do. We aren't our behavior. We are responsible for the impact of our behavior. More to the point, do we like who we are and whom we're becoming? I believe relationship is a spiritual practice. Our relationship with ourselves is a process of self-discovery. To like someone is to feel admiration for them. What do you admire about yourself?

It is easy for us to think of people we like. There are those we do and those we don't. It is as simple as that. The process of sorting "like" and "don't like" is often done in an instant, often without much conscious thought.

There was a time when I couldn't bear the thought that someone might not like me. In conversation, I would become the person I thought they wanted me to be. I molded myself into the desired shape, agreed with the popular point of view, and acted blandly pleasant so as not to cause offense. This made it difficult for people to find me objectionable.

The energy I put into this regimen was enormous. I was certain people wouldn't like me if I showed them my true self and the thought of that crushed me. The irony was that at the end of the day I didn't like myself, because I wasn't being me.

This all changed for me one day when someone brought to my attention that there were people *I* didn't like. Why was it that everyone had to like me, yet it was okay for me not to like everyone? This was my double standard. This was my life, filled with double standards. I knew people who could say no. I couldn't. I knew people who could cry and get angry. I couldn't.

When I inquired more deeply into my own thinking and acting, I discovered several things.

One was that my perceptions of people's disapproval of me were linked to the pain I felt as a kid. When my behavior was disapproved of back then, I turned it into the fact that it was I who was being disapproved of. I made it completely personal. I wasn't good enough. Therefore, later in life, if I even imagined that someone disapproved of me, I rolled my behavior and myself into one odious being that they disliked. So my mandate was to constantly modify my behavior to suit the popular vote.

The next part of the process was to ask, "What's not to like about me?" As I examined myself, I believed I was a good person who did good things. I treated people well, I was honorable, and I told the truth, most of the time!

At this point the double standard reared its head again. The truth was that the only reason someone else couldn't like me would be for the same reasons I didn't like myself, including that I sometimes:

- said yes when I really wanted to say no
- wasn't truthful all the time
- wasn't good to myself
- didn't honor myself
- was a fake
- was resentful
- was angry on the inside, smiling on the outside through gritted teeth.

I could go on, but you get the picture. I was a good person struggling with my self-esteem and my perception of whether or not I could ever tell the whole truth.

Our need to be liked causes us not to like ourselves. Deep down we know we're betraying who we really are. One of the harshest and most shaming statements we can be told, or can tell another, for that matter, is, "You're selfish." That comment is usually lobbed our way when we won't do something the other wants us to do — or, worse, expects us to do. True selfishness is when we expect another to do something because we believe it is the best thing for them. Many people have collapsed the notions of being selfish and being self-centered. They are not the same. When we're centered in our self, we will do the right thing for our self as well as being attentive to the impact of our behavior on the other.

To love someone and not tell the truth is foolish. To tell the truth and be unloving is brutality.

Other people may not like us when we're honest with them, yet they will be able to trust that we will speak our mind and they will know where they stand with us. Now *that* is likability.

Think of people you like. What do you admire about them? Do you like what they do or is your attraction to them centered on who they are being in the world? This distinction is crucial as you focus on your own development. We can and do get stuck in thinking about what we have to do in order to fit in and be liked.

I believe we spend more time looking for how we're different from each other than how we're the same. The usual exception is when we're first attracted to someone: At that point we look for the ways we are the same. This is only momentary (though it may last a few years in some cases) because the brain, given the passage of time, eventually starts to focus on differences.

It is not an either-or situation. Sameness and differences are just perspectives to help us distinguish information. Both are important and useful. The distinctions lose their usefulness when judgment is attached to the information. The moment we judge or compare, we lose objectivity, and the only possible result is insecurity or false pride.

If I judge your skills as better than mine or that you come from a better family or part of town, then I'll pull away from you. I mean, why would you want to connect with me if I am inferior to you?

Likewise, if I think I am better than you, I'll keep myself separate and disconnected, telling myself I don't really fit in.

Bottom line, I get to like myself to the degree that I am willing to be honest and live from a place of truth in my life.

> To create movement in your life answer the following question:
>
> **What major transitions have you been through during the past three years and what have you learned about yourself from them?**
>
> To gain a deeper understanding, please go to relationshipexcellence.com to post your thoughts and read responses from others who are also committed to creating relationship excellence.

Trust

> trust
> 1. to rely on somebody or something
> 2. to place something in somebody's care

What is trust? Trust is repeated patterns of expected behavior.

We've all had to grapple with trust in our lives and maybe still do. Who is it that we ultimately need to trust? Given the way most of us have been raised, we have lost touch with our ability to be deeply connected within ourselves. As a result, we don't know how to trust ourselves or what we trust about ourselves.

When we are our word, our word has value and meaning. We instill value in the word through who we are being in the world. We are completely in charge of whether or not another has trust in us. Actions speak louder than words.

Most of us have a list of people we don't trust for one reason or another. The most important person with whom to develop trust is ourselves. When I can count on myself, knowing without a shadow of a doubt that I will be my word, then I'm developing the stability and groundedness of trust in myself.

How many times have we given our word to another and not kept it? Yet keeping our word is the easiest process to engage in because we're in complete control of the outcome. It is up to us at any given moment. The easiest way to keep our word is to give it less often and to commit to something only when we're willing to follow through on it. We need to look at what prevents us from keeping our word. When we drop the ball on our commitments, we lose respect for ourselves, and so do others.

In this way the three relationship builders of admiration, trust, and respect are intimately linked. All are impacted when we don't keep our word, as they are when we do keep our word. At any given point, we are contributing to building or destroying trust. The more trust another has in us, the less damage is done when, in our human-ness, we screw up.

Think of trust as a bank account. Every time someone keeps their word and follows through on their actions, they are making deposits to our trust account. To have a high account balance is good, especially in the area of trusting others. The real benefit of a high balance in a trust account is when the other person, in their full humanness, screws up, because a withdrawal from the account doesn't cause it to be overdrawn.

What matters is how we clean up any mess we make. When we're impeccable in keeping our word, we function without fault or blame. Being impeccable means taking full responsibility for our part in something. This is how we build trust.

Many years ago I was a college professor. I could see that my colleagues and I were breeding mediocrity by letting students hand their assignments in late. Some students would calculate how late they could hand in the assignment by their grade point average and how many marks they would forfeit by being late.

I decided to take a different approach with my students. I outlined the exact dates on which their assignments were due. I told them I expected them to hand in their assignments on time — or before the deadline, if they wished — and that they had one opportunity to renegotiate the due date. They could call me up to one day before an assignment was due and renegotiate the date. I wasn't open to hearing any reasons or excuses, simply the new date. If they failed to hand in the assignment on the agreed on date, they would get zero marks for the assignment.

My students were very uncomfortable with this new arrangement, because it blocked them from making excuses for their behavior. I was committed to supporting them in becoming aware of the impact of their word on others and on themselves. Ultimately they got to feel the positive impact of keeping their word.

It is fair to say that almost everyone has "trust issues." Most people could easily list the people they trust and the ones they don't. If we take a deeper look at a relationship with one person, we may see how in some areas we trust them while in other areas we don't. We have made decisions about some people because of our direct experience of them, and about others because of what we may have been told about them. It was only in adulthood that I realized that I had learned who my father was through my mother because my father was absent most of my early years. Her view of him was my reality and it had a significant impact on how I experienced him.

I once worked with a woman who couldn't (read *wouldn't*) say no to anyone. She was always running hard doing things for others. She agreed to so much more than she possibly do. Inevitably, she let people down, coming up with creative excuses and promising to make good on her word, starting the cycle all over again. Her real impact was twofold: Others grew not to trust her, and she grew not to trust herself. She imploded on herself because she was filled with self-judgment and self-hatred.

I believe half of what people say and all of what they do. That's the bottom line. What matters are the actions we take and the impact we have in the world. We can know we're in a problematic situation when words and actions don't match. We're always looking for congruity between the two. The real issue is why we put up with incongruent behavior. What do we get from going along with this behavior?

If I challenge you to keep your word, I unconsciously give you permission to do the same with me. The main reason people let others off the hook is that they want the same latitude for themselves. Yet we think we have permission to complain about someone else's untrustworthiness. When we see this in another it is an opportunity to look at our own behavior and become scrupulous in seeking out our own inconsistencies.

In my experience, the feminine will hold the masculine to his word. A woman will hold a man to his word because she wants to trust him. If she is met with resistance, denial, defense, or justification, she will simply lose respect. Men need other men to hold them to a higher standard of trust. Sadly, this is missing in most men's lives. We don't have the right to hold another to a standard that we aren't willing to uphold for ourselves.

The road to hell is paved with good intentions. The challenge is that we judge others by their behavior and judge ourselves by our intentions. The interesting thing about intentions is that they're invisible. We cannot see them in another person. What we see is their behavior and we are left with our interpretation of their behavior.

When I come across couples with a level of connection that I admire, I ask them what works for them. I recall talking to a man who had been married for almost forty years. He and his wife seemed well connected in their behavior. They appeared to be truly enjoying their marriage. Jim told me that soon after they were married, he realized that Margot from time to time seemed hurt in the relationship. Her hurt was linked to his behavior, yet he knew he had never set out to hurt her. He also realized that there had been times when he had felt hurt in the relationship; because of the love they felt for each other he couldn't imagine that Margot had ever set out to hurt him.

Jim said he decided that while he wouldn't take Margot's hurt and pain personally, he would attend to her with all the love he had for her and attempt to understand her pain. He soon discovered that her pain was usually the result of a misunderstanding or misinterpretation of his actions or inaction. Together they found a way to work through the inevitable pain that arose from being in a relationship. Their choice to hang out in the pain created great healing. Consequently their love and appreciation grew and their relationship became a soothing respite from the challenges of day-to-day life.

I know a couple in which both are in their second marriage. They were given two beautiful crystal glasses as a wedding present. They have an agreement that when either of them removes these glasses from the cupboard, it is a signal for them to sit down and resolve whatever issue is present for them. The power here is in the agreement; the glasses are a symbol of that agreement.

I recall hearing about a problem student during a faculty meeting when I was a professor. Many of my colleagues shared their negative experiences and fears about this student along with predictions that those of us yet to encounter him were going to dislike this malcontent, too. I stood up and challenged the status quo. It was true that I had yet to encounter this young student, I said, but perhaps there wasn't such a thing as a problem student, only students whose needs weren't being met. It was our role as teachers to assist this student in better determining his needs and ultimately meeting them.

This didn't win me a popularity contest, but they knew where I stood and I felt better about myself. The same is true in relationship. To some degree, behavior reflects whether our needs are being met.

Each of us has had experiences growing up that have shaped our lives in some way. We might judge them as good or bad. Good or bad are simply labels that judge our experience. As I have mentioned, it is our judgments that cause us to make up stories we then live from. These stories inevitably contribute to our misery, because it is rare that we concoct a story with a happy ending.

Respect

re·spect
  1. to feel or show admiration and deference toward somebody or something
  2. to pay due attention to and refrain from violating something
  3. to show consideration or thoughtfulness in relation to somebody or something

I have heard people say, "I demand that you respect me." You might as well hurl your head against a wall; it will hurt less. Respect cannot be demanded. It can be commanded, but only through offering it to others.

For years I have asked couples to write out what respect means to them. The meaning they give to the word is always different. It is important to know what respect means to you and how you experience respect in the world. What respect means to your partner is likely to be very different. Ask the question. Conduct an inquiry between you into what respect means and looks like in your relationship. Write out when, how, and under what circumstances you feel respected and also how you demonstrate respect. It's a wonderful conversation to have.

I recall thinking as the vows were completed during my first wedding, when I was all of twenty years old: "I have just promised to honor, love, and cherish this woman till death do us part. I have no clue what that means." I never actually told this to anyone until long after my marriage had dissolved. I was clueless about the scale of the commitment I had made. I also never thought until eight years into the marriage that she had made the same promise and that I had no idea what it meant to feel honored, loved, and cherished. We had never discussed it all the years we were married. No wonder we didn't make it. I didn't know how to respect myself because of my family training and a lack of self-awareness.

We use language to describe our experience of life. Just because we use the same word doesn't mean we share the same meaning. We imbue words with meanings that in many cases go way beyond their dictionary definitions. We also use words without any real connection to their actual meaning. For instance, the literal meaning of the word *sarcasm* is *the tearing of flesh* and yet we use sarcasm as humor. No wonder it is so painful.

Rules of engagement are necessary in a relationship to create a safe structure for any couple and family. The problem in most families is that rules don't apply equally to all members in the group. This is where relationship most often breaks down.

In my coaching practice I have a twenty-four-hour cancellation policy. If clients are unable to provide me with twenty-four hours' notice of cancellation and I can fill the session from a waiting list, then they aren't charged. If I'm unable to fill their session time, I ask them to pay for the time booked. Eventually I started applying the policy to myself. If I cancel a session with a client and I'm unable to give them twenty-four hours' notice, I pay them for the session. To me, their time is as valuable as mine. I don't ever ask a client to do something I haven't already done or am not currently doing. None of us has that right.

> To create movement in your life, answer the following question:
>
> **What relationship rules would you like to create that would increase your freedom?**
>
> To gain a deeper understanding, please go to relationshipexcellence.com to post your thoughts and read responses from others who are also committed to creating relationship excellence.

I recall a story about a woman taking her diabetic son to see Gandhi. She asked for an audience with him and waited for him. When she entered with her son, Gandhi asked her why she was there. She explained that her son was diabetic and wouldn't stop eating candy. She was worried about him and knew if Gandhi told him to stop, he would listen. Gandhi thanked her and asked them to leave and return in two weeks.

At the meeting two weeks later, Gandhi asked her again why she was there. She explained again that her son was diabetic and wouldn't stop eating candy.

Gandhi turned to the boy and said, "Listen to your

mother. Stop eating candy." Then he thanked them and asked them to leave.

The mother turned to Gandhi and asked why he hadn't told her son this two weeks earlier.

"First of all I had to stop eating candy," Gandhi replied.

Conclusion

IF YOU ARE WAITING FOR permission to step into your life fully, don't wait any longer. Give yourself permission. Each of us is responsible for setting the tone for the relationship and for pouring into the relationship exactly what it is we hope to create.

This is the law of relationship reciprocity: You get from the relationship what you give to the relationship. When you choose to work on your relationship, not in it, you will be rewarded with an experience of joy and wonderment beyond anything you could have ever imagined.

Remember, there are no sides in relationship, there is just the entity that both of you are responsible for co-creating. The goal is to get out of your own way and create a movement worth joining.

The Powerful Questions

- What is present in your life? Conflict, loneliness, stagnation? In what way are you committed to this result?
- What would you have to resolve within yourself in order for your relationship to operate with a sense of ease?
- What emotional baggage from your family of origin is blocking you in your current relationship?
- How can you invite your partner to join you in co-creating relationship excellence when they don't feel ready to do so?
- What, from your perspective, is the collusion at play in your relationship that is causing both of you to be less than your best?
- How would you describe the dance of your relationship? Be sure to include your steps as

well as your partner's (from your perspective).

o In what way do you punish your partner for not living up to your relationship rules?

o What rules from your family system are you stuck in, causing you to get in your own way?

o What "life sentence" has banished you from fully living your life and relationship?

o What are you unwilling to say no to and what impact is that having on your life?

o What is the writing on the wall that you are refusing to read in your relationship?

o How do you express anger and what is it costing your relationship?

o What unfinished business do you need to clean up? What's keeping you from doing so?

o What insecurity is keeping you from entering fully into your relationship?

o When did you first consider yourself to be a man?

o What is your biggest fear as a man?

o What ways do you try to change your man even though you know from experience that they're not going to work?

o How have you taken your partner for granted in the past?

o What five things would you like to change about yourself that would have you be more content?

○ What are the non-negotiables in your relationship?

○ What truth would you share in your relationship if you felt free to do so?

○ What have you been unwilling to tell the truth about in relationship and what has prevented you from doing so?

○ What truth is the most challenging for you to acknowledge?

○ What major transitions have you been through during the past three years and what have you learned about yourself from them?

○ What relationship rules would you like to create that would increase your freedom?

Additional Resources

I AM ALWAYS CURIOUS ABOUT what works for people. If you are aware of or come across resources that you have found inspiring and supportive on your relationship journey, do send them on to me so they can be listed on our Website.

For the best in resources for men, women, families, and relationships worldwide, go to relationshipexcellence.com/ resources

Listed below are some organizations that I recommend:

The Mankind Project
mkp.org
The Coaches Training Institute
thecoaches.com/
ORSC
centerforrightrelationship.com
Hoffman Institute International
quadrinity.com

About Inner Directions —
The Centre for Relationship Excellence

We are committed to being of service through coaching women and men who want to develop mastery in their lives. The world needs Leadership, families need Leadership, and Relationship needs Leadership. There are no problems that need to be solved; there are only opportunities from which we can grow. We are exactly where we need to be right now. Our resistance to what is is our work in this world.

As my mother used to say, "If you cannot be grateful for what you have, why would God send you more?" When we have lost our gratitude we have lost so much. When we have stopped playing at the Game of Life, it is all chores. Get serious and lighten up!

When you are ready to get out of your own way and risk relinquishing your ego in service of Excellence in the world, contact info@relationshipexcellence.com

Ready to be coached into Relationship Excellence? Contact us as we have an association with twenty CTI Certified Coaches worldwide who are committed to supporting individuals and couples.

Inner Directions —
The Centre for Relationship Excellence
1560 Queen Street East, Suite 202
Toronto, ON M4L 1E9 • (416) 694-0015
relationshipexcellence.com

About Owen Williams

Owen Williams is the founder and director of Inner Directions — The Centre for Relationship Excellence, in Toronto, Canada. He leads a busy coaching practice in Toronto and coaches clients internationally via the phone or through video conferencing.

Owen Williams was born and raised on a farm in Wales. He worked as a classically trained chef and as a senior manager for twelve years in the hospitality industry. For six years he was a professor of Hotel Management at a community college in Toronto. He has had the privilege of working as a Relationship Coach for the past fifteen years through Inner Directions.

Owen has led men's groups and intensives for more than a decade and was awarded the Ron Hering Award in 2008 by The Mankind Project in recognition of his service to men within his community. He co-hosted his own radio show for men and is now working on his own Internet-based radio/television show about relationship. Check out relationshipexcellence.com for show details. Owen has a channel on YouTube with a variety of relationship videos. Go to youtube.com/bwhouare

As a keynote speaker and presenter, Owen gives inspiring and educational talks on relationships and Leadership and facilitates a wide range of workshops for men and women. He offers a range of dialogues on the aspects of relationship that we each need to address in order to create change.

Owen has been married twice and now for the first time thinks he knows what he is doing. He believes that divorce needs to be taken off the table in order for us to commit to the process of being in relationship. While there is a natural rhythm to relationship, there are times when people part ways. Relationships, though, never end; they simply change form. He believes that when this change happens, the two people involved need to honor the relationship for what it was and bless each other as they move on in the journey of life.

To sign up for *The Gift of a Question* newsletter, go to relationshipexcellence.com/newsletter

Printed in the United States
220087BV00001B/2/P